BEING WEST KILBRIDE

Volume 1, 2015

By

Stephen Brown

Published by

The Transparent Publishing Company

www.TransparentPublishing.co.uk

Paperback ISBN 9781909805347
Kindle Version ISBN 9781909805354

First published November 2015

Original Copyright holder – Stephen Brown

CONTENTS

ACKNOWLEDGEMENTS

This book would not at all have been possible except by the incredible interest and enthusiasm of the people of West Kilbride – past and present. It is an honour and deep, deep pleasure to live in West Kilbride and to suddenly be able to reconnect with so many of the people that I have grown up with.

This book must also acknowledge the fantastic tool that Facebook is, and how it has brought so many people together at once in a community conversation that could never have happened in this way in any previous generation.

FIND US ON FACEBOOK:

https://www.facebook.com/groups/WestKilbride/

DEDICATION

TO MY LATE FATHER AND MOTHER WITHOUT
WHOM I WOULD NEVER HAVE LIVED IN
WEST KILBRIDE AND TO MY SISTER AND MY WIFE,
WHO KEEP ME SANE WHILE I DO SO.

INTRODUCTION

Dearie dearie me, I never expected the response I got when I started to load up a few old postcards of my home village as a talking point on Facebook.

I live in the best place in the world – West Kilbride. That is pretty much fact since we have, as a community won so many awards in the last fifteen years, such as "Enterprising Britain", "Creative Places, Scotland" and now as I write we are waiting to hear if we are the top finalist of three villages in the "Great British High Street". We have a huge multimillion pounds project entitled "Craft Town Scotland" of which I had the honour of being Finance Director of for a number of years, an environment group, a fantastic Village Hall, Community Centre, Primary School and two marvellous churches. Our community of some 5000 strong, you will gather is highly motivated and have been for some generations, but our property prices reflect the beauty and desire to be here. Throughout the years, I have sat on many of the committees in the village and continue to try to do my best to see it thrive.

West Kilbride comprises of three main areas – West Kilbride, Seamill, Portencross and Hunterston - each of them absolutely gorgeous. My father came from Portencross, moved to West Kilbride and when I was a boy we lived in houses in West Kilbride and Seamill.

For almost forty years I have gathered a huge collection of postcards of the village. When prices were relatively cheap, I also gathered all manner of other objects, books and papers – in fact anything that had any connection to do with my home town (actually, I am a bit of a collector in general – particularly of the unusual and my whole collection is called the "Yerton Collection" because I am "over the hill"!). I called the West Kilbride part of my collection "Being West

Kilbride" because I felt it spoke to me about what it meant to have been in West Kilbride all through the ages.

In late October 2015, I decided to load a few images from my postcard collection on to a Facebook Group, which I naturally called "Being West Kilbride". At first, I intended running a website in tandem with the Facebook page, but with the rapid growth of the Facebook page, I ran put of time and energy.

People in the hundreds started joining the Facebook Group and as I write this there are almost 1500 members. They are all keen to share memories, communicate with lost friends, marvel at the history of the village and reminisce. I have been overwhelmed with messages of goodwill and support (see some of the "reviews" at the back of this volume). Much of the support comes form a huge group of ex-pats who have a deep seated longing to be home again – our worldwide Facebook Group is just perfect for them.

One of the fascinating issues of the Facebook Group is that it is encouraging people of all generations to take an interest in their home or adopted village. I have had many messages from young people and indeed have been invited to address Primary School Class 6 later this month. The older generation too have been sending me messages of encouragement, and this was one of the reasons why I wanted to write this volume. I am concerned that some of the very much older generation may be missing out on some of the subjects we are discussing, yet they are likely to have most of the inherited wisdom. I am therefore producing this book to keep the technologically challenged up to date with the historical pieces I am sharing with the Facebook Group – in the hope that they will communicate any errors I am making or give me any further information they may have.

But I am also hoping that this book will serve as a reminder to people going forward of some of the topics of local history we have covered. Although I try to archive as much information as possible in Facebook photo albums and file uploads, there are always articles or information missed. Facebook does tend to push things down to the bottom when nobody is interested and this is not always ideal when one is trying to maintain the thread of a discussion. At the moment I am working on an indexing system for the group and hopefully that will resolve this issue.

So, as a catch up, here is Volume 1 of "Being West Kilbride", I hope you enjoy and are encouraged to join the ever growing community on Facebook.

Stephen Brown,
West Kilbride,
November 2015

Defining West Kilbride: "Being West Kilbride" - what does it mean?

Early in the life of the Facebook Group, I asked what "Being West Kilbride" meant to everyone. There was an overwhelming warm response suggesting that it meant a real sense of community- across the divides of geography, age, and wealth. In addition, we also received these comments, al of which I agree:

"a nice wee place to live"
"Insular"
'It's in the heart and on the mind'□

From the growth of the Facebook Group, and the level of activity that I have seen on it, I have no doubt about the community aspect of "Being West Kilbride". There is a fantastic, genuine warmth and a real sense of togetherness.

I too moved away to another country for some years, but felt the tug of home very badly. Whenever I load up a new set of images or historical detail to the site, it is the ex-pats who are often the first to respond. There is a love of the home town like no other, and one that is so hard to describe. Of course as an active member of the SNP, I understand it totally from a political perspective, or when we lose a football match on our way to the World Cup it can be quantified in terms of upset, but I genuinely had not expected the incredible response I had from the outset of this little project.

The Rev Ross Mitchell supplied the quote that it is in the heart and on the mind and I wonder if there could be a joining of the two ideas to say we are "a community in the heart and on the mind".

A History of West Kilbride in 100 Objects: The Souvenir Spoon

Who can forget the Souvenir Spoon? How many of us have vast collections of spoons up the attic that were collected by travelling parents or grandparents? Of course, most are worthless nowadays, unless they happen to be silver.

In West Kilbride, the Souvenir Spoon has been a stalwart of the Main Street trade for a century. You can still buy them in the D&B Gallery in West Kilbride. The spoon in the picture is the earliest I have ever found.

This is a silver spoon, hallmarked for Birmingham 1916. It would not have been a souvenir for the general mincers like myself (the hoi polloi, the great unwashed or the sans-cullotes if you will). No, no, this would have been for the more refined visitor to our fair shores - one that might have been kept for a gentleman's cabinet.

(If you have ever wondered why the highest political committee is called a "cabinet" it is because of the Victorian tradition that a gentleman's closest friends were his cabinet. On dark winter nights, after dinner had been served, a gentleman's cabinet might retire for port and cigars and to study the latest antiquarian finds or collectable item of the host.)

The town crest on the spoon is of course, the accepted W.H. Goss "official" one. By 1916, there were several other crests appearing on the Main Street (see my excellent book "The West Kilbride Town Coat of Arms". We may never know who might have ordered the manufacture of this one – was it the Todd Brothers, who by now were the main outlet for this sort of thing? Could it have been a trial by Goss themselves, whose factory was relatively near Birmingham?

It is often hard to imagine, but our little village was, at the start of the 20th Century, one of the most popular places to visit in Scotland. We were about the second or third village to get a W.H. Goss town crest and all the souvenir crested wares that came with it. Hence the reason why there are so many designs which I will shortly be illuminating.

But where the crested china was cheap and nasty for the bulk tourist market, a silver spoon was not. The fact that the date of manufacture was 1916 was another clue in my search to dispel the original town crest had been designed by Jay Lascelles, the Head of Art in Ardrossan Academy in the late 1920's. When I acquired this spoon plus a number of early postcards showing the crest, and also the earliest W.H. Goss crested china pieces, it all fell into place.

But in my humble opinion, the souvenir spoon, is one of the "History of West Kilbride in 100 Objects" because it has amongst us for 100 years and many of us knew so little about it. This is the finest example I have seen to date.

Derivation of Place Names: Definitions

The Rev. John Lamb in his second book published in 1899 describes three "principles of nomenclature classification" for places and street names in and around our West Kilbride. Over the last 110 years, there has been a huge amount of development within the village and its surrounds. I believe that we must now extend this definition to six principle nomenclature categorisations as below. The first three are from Lamb, and the second three are my humble attempt to update his list.

1. Position – for example Meadowfoot, Glenfoot, Castle View;
2. Proprietorship – such as Hunterston, Boydston;
3. Ecclesiastical – considering such names as Kilbride, Kilruskin;
4. Renames – where areas have been renamed for whatever reason, for example Ridshiels became Bowfield, Burrough Faulds became Pantonville;
5. External geographical references such as Snowdon, Avondale, Merlewood; and
6. Topographical references such as Knock Georgan meaning "hill of reeds"

When I describe the derivations of names on Facebook, I always have these six categories at the back of my mind when I am trying to establish form whence a place name came. Earlier works on these matters such as Lamb or Isaac Jackson have been rather fanciful when it comes to explaining derivations, and this has caused a huge divergence in the analysis of local history, from the truth.

For example, local historians since the Old Statistical Account (1799) have defined Portencross as the "Port of the Cross" in some fashion or other. From there we have had conjectures, accepted as truths, such as the Templars must have visited us, or that the dead kings of Scotland were transported to Iona from here. There is no evidence of that of course. Whereas the simpler explanation is that it is simply the "port of Crosbie" since the port was in older times on that extensive estate. It is therefore very important to cast down the list above in order to not evoke fanciful notions before eliminating the obvious.

Derivation of Place Names: Gateside Street

This one I had to use a little lateral thinking a wee bit, for it is not that the street is beside a gate. It is however, beside Caldron Hill.

In Pont's map of 1604, Caldron Hill is listed as Cadrongatle - all one word. This probably should have been the ancient celtic "Cader" meaning "the seat of". Isaac Jackson suggests that this may have come from the Welsh who, according to Geoffrey of Monmouth, lead by Cadwallo clattered through Albany on their way to Hibernia - but I think relating Cadron to Cadwallo this may be a little fanciful. So the best guess we have really for the first part of the name "Cadron" may mean "seat of".

The second part of the name "gatle" is supposed to be possibly the name of a local chieftain. I have seen it suggested that "gatle" is an old Scotls word for garrison or army camp - which has led some to speculate that this might have been the spot where the Roman General Agricola brought his 30,000 German auxiliaries to, when attempting to invade Ireland in AD81. However, no evidence has been found of this, and although there is the usual sprinkling of Roman finds on the grounds of Gateside, there is nothing to suggest such huge numbers.

So what I am hereby proposing is that Gateside is actually simply "Gatle Side"

Derivation of Place Names: Biglees

The original name of this part of the Southannan estate was "Beyglies". Nevertheless, it was pronounced locally as "Biglees". Beyglies is Anglo Saxon meaning large pastures or fields.

Having earlier read about Norse, Middle English, Lowland Scots, Irish Gaelic, Medieval French, Norman and Scottish Gaelic influences on the place names of West Kilbride, now we find an Anglo-Saxon reference. Shortly in this series, we shall also even be joined by the Welsh.

Anglo Saxon farmers would have been in all likelihood, brought to Scotland by the Normans as vassals. The Norman nobles (such as Richard De Horssey of Horse Island fame) usually had substantial land holdings in England and would have used the Anglo Saxons as feudal labourers.

History: Crosbie Tower

Crosbie Tower is a small fortalice of probable early 17th century date, somewhat altered in the second half of the same century, and with a larger modern mansion added. It is L-shaped here, consisting of a main block, of two storeys, an attic, and a garret in height, with a stair wing projecting at the SW end rising a storey higher. The building is very plain, many windows have been enlarged, and there are no gunloops or turrets. There was a much earlier tower on the site, which Pont describes, and which was largely taken down and rebuilt after his visit. The NSA (1845) mentions restoration work being carried out in 1837. The original entrance in the SW face of the staircase tower has been converted into a window, above it the lintel of a smaller window bears the date 1676. Another tablet bears the date 1896, probably the date of the additions. The house at this time was in good condition and was used as a youth hostel.

Crosbie is as described, and is now privately owned. There was a modern plaque by the entrance stating that the tower remains are 17th century and adds that "(it) occupies the site of a much earlier tower belonging to the Crauford family. William Wallace, the Scottish patriot, is thought to have had sanctuary here with his uncle Reginald Crauford".

The buildings at risk register states: T plan, consisting of a crow-stepped gabled oblong with projecting staircase tower having a small watchroom at the top; 3 storeys and attic; door is in the west side of the tower. Restored in late 19th century and originally contained some good chimneypieces and panelling.

In 2007, due to storm damage, the building was partially demolished and the remains now stand in Crosbie Towers Caravan Park.

Transcripts: In Ayrshire: A Descriptive Picture of The County of Ayr; *William Scott Douglas (1874)*

West Kilbride

This parish is bounded on the north by that of Largs; on the east by Dalry and Ardrossan; and on the west and south-west by the firth of Clyde. Directly opposite the centre of the coast-line lies the island of Little Cumbrae, which (*quoad sacra*) is attached to West Kilbride. The name is obviously derived from St. Bride, a holy virgin in the Scotch calendar of Romish Saints; and a fair called "Bridesday," formerly held on the 1st February, and now about twelve days thereafter, has immemorially taken place in the village.

The greatest length of the parish is six miles, and its greatest breadth four; but its general figure being triangular, or rather almond shaped, measures not more than a mile wide at either end, while the sea-line on the west extends about eight miles. A great rocky promontory in the central part of the coast line is shaped like the hunch on a dromedary's back, and measures two-and-a-quarter miles from north to south, by one and a quarter in breadth. This promontory is terminated in the south-west corner by the ruins of Portincross Castle, built on a rocky peninsula, and is crowned by a celebrated precipice called in old writings "Goldberrie Head," and now usually styled Ardneil Bank.

This majestic natural wall, rising in some parts to 300 feet of perpendicular rock, is carried in a straight line along the water's edge, from which it is separated only by a narrow slip of green land, and extends to at least a mile in length. At its base the precipice is richly fringed with natural coppice, in which the ash, the oak, hazel, and hawthorn, are thickly interwoven; and farther up, grey lichens intermixed with ivy, and varied with large patches of golden-coloured vegetation, climb the steeps almost to the topmost heights. The general mass of these stupendous rocks consist of dark-red sandstone in horizontal position; but about midway up, the sandstone is surmounted by beautiful brown porphyry. This part of the precipice is divided into three deeply separated cliffs of equal height and uniform appearance which have long received the name of the "Three Sisters," or the "Three Jeans," as the sailors prefer to call them. In the statistical description of West Kilbride, drawn by the late John Fullarton, Esq., an heritor in the parish, he says in regard to these cliffs, that "viewed from the plain below, the effect is highly impressive and sublime; whilst to approach their terrific summit, the vivid description by Shakspeare of the Cliff of Dover is fully realised.

Ardneil Bay lies to the south of the promontory just described. This is a beautiful sandy crescent now lotted out for feuing purposes, affording an agreeable promenade and easy access for bathing to those who enjoy that healthful recreation. Farther south, until the adjoining parish is reached, there are several similar bays of smaller dimensions. The higher portions of the parish lying to the north and east of the great promontory, embrace the properties of Southannan and Crosby, which were disjoined from Largs about 1650, and annexed to Kilbride. On the other hand the lands of Monfode, Knockewart, and Boydston, originally forming the southern and eastern part of West Kilbride, were at the same time cut off and annexed to Ardrossan, the latter only *Quoad sacra*.

Tradition asserts that on the hill of Goldberry, at the time of the Norwegian invasion, a detachment of the army of Haco was attacked and routed by a body of Scots, led by Sir Robert Boyd, progenitor of the Kilmarnock family, and from this some suppose they added the "Goldberry" as a motto on their shields. Along the banks facing the sea-beach, particularly at Boydston, Glenhead, and Seamill, are seen a chain of little eminences called "Castle Hills," supposed to be the remains of a primitive class of fortlets.

These are placed at unequal distances, from half-a-mile to a mile-and-a-half apart all constructed in the same manner, and of very limited dimensions. Conjecture assigns these structures to the era of the Danish incursions; but they may belong to a still higher antiquity. The Castle of Portincross, long a seat of the Boyd family, is still somewhat entire, although it has for ages been in a ruinous condition. The early Stuart Kings in passing to Dundonald and Rothesay, were wont to cross the channel at this point, and occasionally rest, it is said, within its walls; but whether this refers to the old castle on the top of the *auld hill*, the foundation of which may still be traced, is a question not easily solved. Some royal charters exist bearing to have been signed at "Ardnele."

One of the large ships of the Spanish armada of 1588, after the dispersion of that formidable fleet, having found her way into the firth of Clyde, ultimately perished close to the old castle. One iron cannon, out of many, recovered from the sunken vessel, still lies on the beach at Portincross: this estate now belongs to E. H. J. Craufurd of Auchinames, who has an elegant cottage near the old castle.

The inhabitants of the northern parts of Ayrshire appear to have had a considerable share as sufferers in the unhappy carnage of Pinkie, in 1547. From Kilbride, the lairds of Hunterston and Monfode, with many of their tenantry, fell in the fray. At Langside also, Robert Boyd of Portincross, with great numbers from this quarter, were present on the Queen's side. The offence thereby given to the successful party seems soon to have been remitted, and the Boyds taken into favour; for the whole of the church lands here were shared between the "Good Earl of Glencairn," and Lord Boyd.

There were not many of the natives of this parish who joined the Covenanters during the times of the persecution, but during the strict times which preceded it, the minister of Kilbride, by name George Crawfurd, was deposed by his presbytery "for worldly mindedness, and for selling a horse on the Sabbath day," Robert Boyd of Portincross, was one of the witnesses against him in the cause.

The parish-town, or village, lies in a finely-sheltered position on the Kilbride burn, in an agricultural district about half-a-mile from the beautiful sea-beach. Its population is 1,218, and that of the whole parish only 1,880: the industries carried on seem to be divided between agricultural pursuits and hand-loom weaving, together with muslin sewing.

For a long time after the Union settlement, in consequence of the dearth of profitable employment, the inhabitants of the whole coast of Ayrshire devoted themselves greatly to traffic in smuggled brandy and rum, accompanied by its usual demoralizing effects. West Kilbride was no exception to the general rule. The parish contains above 10,000 square acres, nearly one-third of which is waste land, fitted only for pasture, and the natural adaptation of the arable portion of the soil obviously is to dairy purposes. Lime is frequently applied to the soil, but in consequence of the expense of conveyance, is not so commonly used for manure as sea-weed which is abundant, and very effectual when applied in a fresh condition.

Mr. Fullerton, already referred to, remarks that "the chief advantage of which this parish is susceptible, is as a sea-bathing station and coast residence, though hitherto very little has been attempted towards that object. The sea-shore all the way from the fine harbour of Ardrossan to Portincross northward, a reach of five miles, is in all respects peculiarly suitable for such a purpose. Bordering on the wide and open channel with a southern aspect, the beach is finely shelving and accessible; whilst nearly all along, steep and picturesque banks give complete protection from the north and east." It may be noted farther that a new and tastefully laid-out cemetery is to be seen adjoining the village of Kilbride, in the middle of which is a high and chaste Monumental Structure in memory of Dr. Robert Simpson, Professor of Mathematics in Glasgow University, three-fourths of the expense of this monument was contributed by the late John Fullerton of Overton. A new and handsome church with a spire, has also lately been erected in the village on the site of the old church, at a cost of about £3,000. The spire is adorned with an elegant clock, the expense of which was raised by subscription.

The remains of many fine old castles and towers are situated within the parish. Besides that of Portincross already described, there exist the walls of the stately tower of Law castle, quite entire. It is beautifully situated on a steep eminence overlooking the village, and commands delightful prospects of the islands and firth to the westward. Crosby Castle, belonging, with its adjacent grounds, to E. H. J. Crawfurd of Auchinames, is a picturesque object, near which, it is said, existed the original "Tower of Crosby," where Wallace found refuge with his uncle, Sir Ronald Craufurd, during the period of his outlawry. There is another Crosby in Kyle with which this incident has been associated, but apparently in error, for Crosby in

Cunninghame undoubtedly was an inheritance of Craufurd, Sheriff of Ayr, whereas its namesake in Kyle belonged to the Fullertons.

On the estate of Southannan in the northern portion of the parish, the family of Sempil had a splendid mansion, the ruins of which still remain. Lastly may be mentioned the old fortlet of Hunter of Hunterston, the lands of which have been possessed in the same line for several centuries. The modern mansion house and grounds have altogether a very unique and picturesque appearance.

ISLAND OF LITTLE CUMBRAY

This island lies about a mile and a half west of Ardneil Bank, its surface measuring about one and a quarter square miles. Although ecclesiastically attached to West Kilbride, it is politically a portion of the shire of Bute. It rises from 500 to 600 feet above the level of the sea, extends to nearly 700 acres, and is the property of the Earl of Eglinton. An old light-house crowns its summit, and a burying-ground lies eastward nearer the shore. On an islet at the side are still found the remains of a castle, which, during Cromwell's hostile visit to Scotland, was occupied by the Earl of Eglinton as a place of retreat. At the northern point of the island are some large "barrows" (partly opened in 1813), in which were found steel helmets and other remains, bones, &c., supposed of the warriors who fell at the battle of Largs in 1363. The remains of an ancient chapel and tomb of its patron saint, called St. Vey, still exist on the island. For at least a century back the isle has been used chiefly as a rabbit warren, about 450 dozen of which are taken annually. A few sheep and some young cattle occasionally graze upon it.

Defining West Kilbride: The Baronies

The seven baronies or substantial estates in 1874 were properly divided as follows:

Southannan, Ardneil or Portincross, Hunterstoun, Crosby, Kilbryde, Carlung, and Drummilling.

A History of West Kilbride in 100 Objects: The Glenfield Water Fountain

This sorry looking public water fountain, attached to the wall on the main street side of the Barony, behind the bus stop, actually has quite an interesting history. There remain only two known examples still in situ, of which this is one.

Note along the top, the instruction – "Keep the Pavement Dry". The middle text says "T. Kennedy Patentee" and the bottom "Kilmarnock". The fountain is no longer operational and the bowl has been filled with concrete. The mechanisms (see below) at the rear of the fountain have been removed.

Origins

These water fountains were placed all round the Kilmarnock area by the company Glenfield and Kennedy, in the 1860's. They were paid for by local Town Councils.

The picture below is of Thomas Kennedy Snr. Founder of Glenfield & Kennedy

Glenfield and Kennedy had been established in 1852 by Thomas Kennedy Snr who was the inventor of the worlds first water meter (see photo to right).

However the major growth period of Glenfield & Kennedy was

between 1871 and 1904, under the direction of Thomas Kennedy (nephew of Thomas Kennedy, senior). Under his influence 'The glen' became one of the most important hydraulic engineering concern in Britain, with substantial export orders to most parts of the world.

At it's height, the factory of Glenfield & Kennedy operated from 26 acres of land and employed 2,600 people.

Using the discoveries and inventions of his father, Thomas Kennedy Junior developed a range of water meters and equipment that took the company's products worldwide, and eventually the company became one of the world's largest light engineering businesses.

On the right is a photograph of Thomas Kennedy Jnr. Who was the architect of the company's success

Water meters (fluviometers) measure the volume of water passing through them and it was this product, accurate to within one percent that made Glenfield & Kennedy famous throughout the world.

The original fluviometer was designed in 1824 by Thomas Kennedy Snr with the help of local, Kilmarnock, clockmaker John Cameron. Water coming into the meter is directed by a small valve either above or below a piston in a cylinder of known volume. The rise and fall of the piston, apart from expelling the measured quantities of water, also drives a counting mechanism and recording dials.

Our West Kilbride water fountain was one of many, invented and patented by Thomas Kennedy Snr. It was manufactured in Kilmarnock and ordered by the West Kilbride Town Council around the 1860's. It would have been installed on the main street by Glenfield & Kennedy and the nearest we can get to an original photograph in colour is the one shown here.

The water would be drawn by pulling the knob on the top centre of the fountain. Behind the unit was a fluviometer that measured the amount of water taken from the fountain. This would have been set into the barony wall. There has been a suggestion that the height of the fountain set into the wall, was to allow dogs to drink from the bowl at the bottom.

Where are they now?

Glenfield still exists to this day, under the company name of Glenfield Valves Limited. It was acquired by the AVK group in 2001. Since then, design and technologies from other acquired UK valve manufacturers (i.e. Bestobell / Blakeborough, Guest & Chrimes/Saint Gobain) have been incorporated into Glenfield's Product Offer. Then, in 2005/06, major investments into Glenfield Valves Ltd were made, ensuring that we are ready to meet the ever increasing requirements from the Global Water Industry.

Their product portfolio comprises a large and comprehensive range of gate valves, butterfly valves, check and recoil valves as well as a proven and reliable range of submerged discharge valves and free discharge valves for the dams and reservoir industries.

Derivation of Place Names: Weston Terrace

This is fairly straightforward - in the 19th Century, the Surrey based Weston family married into the Hunter of Hunterston family. Their son became Lt Gen Aylmer Hunter Weston - famed for being rather eccentric before, during and after WW1. Weston Terrace was named after this side of the Hunter family.

Derivation of Place Names: Overton (Overton Drive, Overton Church, Overton Court, Yerton Brae)

The original spelling of Overton was actually Overtoun. This signified an estate of land that was physically higher than the main part of the town – which may have been represented by the administrative centre – Kirkton Hall.

On Plot 104 of the Barony Parish Church graveyard, the stone reads:

WOODSYDE
This
Monument
Is erected by me Archibald
Woodsyde in memory of my father Archibald
Woodsyde Farmer
In Overtoun he died 22 Octr
1732 aged 70 years
Also Mary Kyle his Spouse
She died 22 Nov 1719 aged
78 years Also two of my
Children Elizabeth & Robert

By the time we reach the mid 19th Century the estate of Overton (the name had been shortened) was a substantial tract of land stretching approximately from where Overton Church is now, all the way to the Sea. The seat of the estate was Overton House which sat at the Well Street entrance to where Overton Court now starts. Overton House was demolished in the late 1950's to make way for the Overton

Court development. A ground floor flat in Overton Court was my first abode as a child.

The family that owned the Overton estate was the Ritchie family (Ritchie Street).

We first hear of Yerton in the earliest part of the twentieth century. Prior to this, the name Overton had solely been used. Yerton is supposedly middle English meaning "Over the Hill" and would mean the same as Overton which is lowland Scots. In Lamb's second book of 1899 he refers to the Yerton Brae as Seamill Brae, so we may be fairly sure that it was named after that date. However, I have old postcards in my possession from around 1905 showing the name of Yerton Brae. I would conclude therefore that the Brae was simply renamed by property developers.

Derivation of Place Names: Faulds (Faulds Burn, Faulds Wynd, Burough Faulds)

This is lowland Scots meaning "fields". Burough Faulds relates to the area of land from Caldwell Road to the coast and was the former name of Pantonville Road.

History: A Short History of the Todd Brothers Retailers

RBS shut its doors on the 27th October 2015, having been in the Village since 1877, bringing to an end a banking service to our community lasting 138 years. Despite their promises to the contrary when the Clydesdale Bank closed, they have left us a village without a bank. Of course they were not in the same premises all that time, as between 1880 and the 1960's the whole building, upstairs and downstairs was the famous Todd Brother's emporium. The Todd Bros offered a huge list of goods for sale, from ironmongery to animal feed, tourist crested china to newspapers, clothing to bedroom linen.

On the 1907 postcard shown here, the Todd Bros shop is the grey building on the left. The large wooden sign on the side of the next-door building (now Climie's Butchers) detailed all the excellent items that could be purchased.

"True economy procures all things that are necessary, but uses prudent management in the buying. The highest economy may be practised by purchasing here."

I detail the story of the Todd Brothers in my book – the "A History of the Town Coat of Arms" (available on Amazon worldwide), but bring an edited version here for your edification.

The Todd Brothers (John and Alexander Smith) were born to a grocery family in Broomhouse in Lanarkshire – not 12 miles from Avondale where John Dunlop grew up (Avondale Road, Avondale Lodge). John Dunlop, another successful trader in the village, was almost exactly the same age as Alexander Smith Todd, they both arrived in the village at approximately the same time, and both had great aspirations to climb the social ladder. All of this may serve to explain their close friendship.

John Todd was the older brother and was born in 1856 to James Todd and Helen Smith. James Todd was a successful grocer in Lanarkshire. We know very little of John's early life, but find him in 1880 living in West Kilbride in a boarding house having established a small grocers and employing one young assistant.

In 1884, he met Thomasina Allan Henderson from Ardrossan and they were married in 1885. They moved into a house entitled Glen Ariven in West Kilbride (anyone know it?). Soon thereafter, Thomasina fell pregnant and the oldest son James Smith Todd was born in 1887. James would ultimately take over the family business.

As the village grew though massive building works to accommodate the ever growing tourist trade, John Todd found himself in a very busy situation on the Main Street – perhaps as he had planned from the outset. The late 1880's saw the start of a property boom, where large houses were being built in great numbers to make boarding houses, hotels or large seaside residences for the wealthy. There was also a new Co-operative home in Corse Street. John saw the opportunity to supply these large buildings wholesale with all their cleaning materials and hardware supplies, whilst supplying the general public the same items at retail prices on the main street. As the tourists rolled in, through the 1880's John's life had become very busy – a new wife and house, a new baby and a thriving business.

John was a natural businessman, with a great eye for an opportunity, and whilst he was very hard working, even he had limits. In the late 1880's he had witnessed a young man with energy, James Dalzell Simpson, start a newsagent on the main street and expand into highly profitable tourist goods. John was supplying the tourist houses, and the people who lived in West Kilbride, but as yet he had not really considered the high margin tourist trade.

The second son to John and Thomasina was born in 1890 – John Alexander. Even here there is a sense of pending discussions regarding partnership with his beloved brother, Alexander. There is also a sense of frustration when we study the 1891 Census return – John lists his occupation as a "Grocer and Cluna Merchant" ("Cluna" apparently being a lowland Scots word meaning superfluous items).

By 1890 John realised that he needed help to expand the business further. He could see several opportunities to expand, but would have to invest in inventory to do so. He decided to invite his younger Alexander into the business as a junior partner. He knew he could trust Alexander and that he would work hard and cheaply for the business to make it work.

Alexander Smith Todd was six years younger than his brother John and was very much the flamboyant energetic entrepreneurial "front man" to John's Presbyterian work ethic. Together they formed a long lasting retail partnership that was very much a pre-cursor for successful retail traders on the west coast of Scotland – no debt, all available profits re-invested in the business with continued expansion.

Alexander arrived in West Kilbride in 1891 and immediately expanded the business into ironmongery and hardware. He married Kate in 1893 and they had a son, Clark in 1895, and two daughters – Mary in 1896 and Helen in 1898. Kate was not always in the best health and when they moved into a new large house – Maur St. Glensherica (anyone know it?) – they seemed to require the services of two servants.

Meantime, John and Thomasina had several further children – Robert Alexander in 1888, the twins George and William in 1899 and Hilda in 1900, making a grand total of six children for John and three for Alexander.

In 1893, John had also moved house – to an address simply listed as Maur St. Cudenarde (in his death certificate it is spelled Oudenarde). I have no real definitive knowledge of where any of these houses were – perhaps at Ardneil as I believe the two houses there were once referred to as the Mhor. The names of the houses is a mystery – there are several places in the world entitled "Maur" ranging from a hotel in the Isle of Wight, a Canton in Switzerland and indeed a district in the Punjab in India. Oudenarde appears to be a town in Belgium, but as yet I have found no reference to Glensherica or any information that may link these names.

The early 20th Century was extremely busy for the Todd brothers as they sought to consolidate their now much larger shop. They had purchased the whole block (shown in grey on the left in the postcard above) and were steadily increasing inventory.

In late 1906, the opportunity had arisen to enter the crested china market as John Dunlop (Alexander's friend) announced his intention to retire. The main manufacturer in England, William H. Goss had died and other pottery companies offering different products with similar coat of arms were emerging. Alexander approached Swan China and together they designed a new version of the Goss / Simpson coat of arms. I own a large collection of West Kilbride Crested China and will share that with you over time.

What was unique about the Swan / Todd pieces was that each item produced between 1907 and 1909 was stamped underneath with stamp naming the Todd Brothers as "Fancy Dealers". This allows us to date Swan pieces extremely accurately, and makes them extremely rare – only four examples have been found so far. See the photo attachment below.

After 1910, the Todd Brothers were forced to sell Arcadian crested china ware along with all other retailers, with the Arcadian version of the town coat of arms.

Eventually, John's son James took over the business and it continued until the late 1960's when he retired. John Todd died of old age at home in July 1935, aged 78. Alexander latterly went to live with one of his children in Glasgow and died in Kelvingrove in 1940, also aged 78.

The shop then was split into two, becoming A.D. Murray on the right hand side and RBS on the left. A.D. Murray was taken over by Donald Ribbeck who continued the tradition of a general goods store and newsagents for many years until his eventual retirement. Donald continues to work tirelessly for any number of voluntary causes in the village – I enjoyed many a Saturday afternoon with him in the furniture sales in the Barony church before it became the exhibition centre it is today.

Peter Ribbeck, Donald's son, is an internationally renowned landscape photographer, and member of this group. I wholehearted suggest that you become his friend as his photos of the west coast of Scotland are utterly, utterly wonderful – and visit his website of course – www.PeterRibbeck.com.

Transcripts: The Statistical Accounts of Scotland, West Kilbride, Ayrshire, Account (1791-99)

Note: The reason I have included the full transcript of this highly useful historical document is very simply that it is the foundational document from which most other local historians such as Reverend John Lamb, Isaac Jackson or Peter A. MacNab took their "facts". Although the Rev Oughterson was clearly a very learned man of the Parish, he was rather taken to conjecture or expanding on his own fanciful notions – this is possibly the most obvious in the passages relating to Portencross.

It was very clearly in the benefit of the community of West Kilbride and area, and the Rev Oughterson, if the status of the village were somehow raised. The local Barons would also support such conjectures as clearly they would gain through an increase in status and land value.

Our temptation is to believe that because the document is old, and thereby nearest to a "contemporary" record as we can get, then it must clearly all be true. Prior to the invention of the internet, these documents were all that were available, and local historians were lured into often repeating the misconceptions of the Rev Oughterson, giving them further credibility until locally these ideas became known as "fact".

Now with the internet and the huge appetite for research and understanding, coupled with an ever increasing demand for more and more authentic history of our area, we must re-examine these "facts". Being West Kilbride is simply one such vehicle that proposes to do just that. (Stephen Btrown)

Number 31, Parish of West Kilbride
(County of Ayr, Synod of Glasgow and Ayr, Presbytery of Irvine)

By the Rev. Mr Arthur Oughterson

Name, Extent, Surface, &cc.

In the Monkish ages, it was very common for religious recluses, to give names to the places where they either chose to fix their solitary residence, or to have their remains consigned after death. From thence, then name of this parish is obviously derived, being compounded of the Gaelic word "Kile", a burial-place, or the Latin, "Cells," and Bridget, the name of the titular female Saint of the place. This parish is of moderate extent, stretching, in length, from the mouth of the Frith of Clyde, directly N. along the shore, for above 6 English miles. From the promontory of Portincross, to the remotest island parts over the hills, it is about 3 ½ English miles broad; in other places, between 2 and 3 miles. It is bounded upon the whole of the west by the sea and Frith of Clyde. It comprehends in it, the lesser island of Cumbray, which is separated from the main land by a sound 3 miles over. Upon the most eminent part of this island, a light-house was erected, about a year 1750, which hath proved of great benefit to this trade; but from its too lofty situation, it is often so involved in clouds, as not to be perceptible, or, but very dimly seen. The managers have therefore judged it necessary to erect another upon a lower station, upon which is to be placed a reflecting lamp. This will not be liable to the inconvenience attending the other and will afford a more certain direction to vessels navigating the Frith in the night time. This work is now executing, and soon will be completed.

The whole of this parish is a part of that mountainous track of country, which commencing at the southern boundary of it, continues all the way to Greenock. It therefore presents every where, a broken, unequal surface, rising in many places into high hills, interspersed with a number of romantick rivulets, and some of them green to their very summits. From the tops of these hills, a prospect presents itself, which, for variety and grandeur, is scarcely to be equalled. At one view, the eye takes in the broken land and small sounds formed by the islands of Arran, Bute, the two Cumbrays, and the coasts of Cowal and Cantire; the extensive coast of Carrick, from Ayr to Ballintrae ; a wide expanded Frith, with the rock of Ailsa rising majestic in its very bosom; the stupendous rocks and peak of Goatfield in Arran; while the distant cliffs of Jura are seen just peeping over the whole, in the back ground. Such a landscape is exceedingly rare and has always been particularly pleasing to strangers.

Climate, &cc.

From the vicinity of this district to the sea, the air is generally moist and the climate variable; great quantities of rain falling in the spring and autumn, which proves a considerable hinderance to farming operations. Notwithstanding these circumstances, the inhabitants are for the most part healthy, few diseases being epidemical among them; and many of them live to a great age. An example of uncommon longevity occurred some years ago, of a man in the lesser island of Cumbray, who died in the advance period of 101. The diseases most common, are the rheumatism, and what is called the bastard peripneumony, which most frequently attacks old people. Palsies too, sometimes occur. And here it may be proper to observe, that all the different kinds of nervous diseases, are found to prevail more in countries situated upon the shore, than in inland parts. Whether this is to be ascribed to some peculiar quality in the air, that predisposes to these nervous affections, there being no material difference in the manner of living, the writer will not take upon him to determine. A very malignant species of quinsy, vulgarly called the closing, in some seasons, proves fatal to children of between 3 and 5 years of age. It makes its appearance in the spring and autumn and baffles every remedy. The small-pox, when they are of a virulent kind, carry off a good many; and hitherto, all efforts to introduce inoculation have failed. No arguments can overcome the superstitious opinions of the people, or their dread of the popular odium.

Soil, Agriculture, &cc.

As this quarter abounds so much in hills, the soil, upon the whole must be poor, and in many places wet and springy; but to this general description there are exceptions; and there might be still more, were any justice done to the land, or proper attempts made, with judgement and persevering industry, to overcome or alleviate its natural disadvantages. The 3 following soils are the most common: A very light, dry, sandy soil, with a mixture of good earth; the mossy; and a strong tilly clay. These different soils point out to the intelligent farmers, what method of cultivation they would require. It is agreed, that compost of dung, earth and lime, would suit the first mentioned soil; and that when laid down richly, it would produce excellent crops of clover and other grasses; yet this hath never been sufficiently tried : and until of late years, the farmers in this part of the country, who had adopted the very worst practice of the old husbandry, remained utterly unacquainted with the method of laying down land in this manner. However, nature has done a great deal for them here, by affording a spontaneous manure, which is well adapted to the light land, and, in a great measure, supersedes the necessity of any other, and that is sea-weed, which is thrown in in such vast quantities by the winter gales, that the people have only to be at the pains to lead it out and lay it upon their fields. This manure from its hot stimulating nature, is of quick operation, and when aided by a moist summer, and refreshing showers, throws up bountiful crops. For many years, this was the only manure used for general cultivation; and it was applied to all soils indiscriminately, to which it could be transported; and where this was not practicable, the land was left without any other means of improvement, than what it derived from more rest; any little dung made upon the farm, being used for raising potatoes and bear. The method of management for the outfield land of such farms as lie without the reach of sea-weed, is to let it rest for 4 years; then plough it for a scourging crop of oats; then let it rest as before; next succeed the 2 ploughings; and so in this rotation.

For the other 2 soils mentioned, lime is certainly exceeding proper; but very strong prejudices were long entertained against it. When the present incumbent entered to his charge, there was not an ounce of lime laid upon the land within the parish, and no reasoning could prevail with the farmers to try it: they pleaded their ignorance of its operation, the method of applying it, and the great expense attending the conveyance of it from a distant kiln. But, whether from observing the great advantages arising from it in neighbouring parishes, where it hath been long introduced, or that they are subjected to certain regulations by the late leases, or from the more enterprising spirit of some new proprietors, a mighty change has taken place in the people's ideas with regard to lime, in consequences of which, vast quantities of it have been laid upon the land within there 3 years; greater indeed, in proportion to the extent of the parish, than any other within the county. This gives ground to hope that a better method of husbandry, though yet in its infancy, will, in a few years, from perseverance and the influence of a laudable example, become more general.[1]

The crops chiefly raised in this parish, are oats and bear: the quantity produced from an acre, is from 5 to 7 bolls. In strong clean land, flax succeeds well, and for a reason which will hereafter be mentioned, the attention of the people hath been much turned to the cultivation of the plant, and greater quantities of flax are raised in Kilbride, than in any neighbouring district; it is most commonly sown after potatoes. The soil being peculiarly adapted to potatoes, they produce luxuriantly. Whet is seldom sown here, and no attempts hitherto made to introduce it into general practice, have succeeded to expectation. Beans and pease are not much cultivated; for, besides that, the soil in most places is reckoned too light for them; in a climate where the weather and seasons are so variable. They are, not without reason, considered as a hazardous crop. One circumstance, which ought not to be omitted, in describing the state of agriculture in this parish, is, the improved taste some proprietors have discovered of late, in the constructing of steadings, or farm-houses, up on their estates: in place of the old dirty, cold, inconvenient huts, the tenants are now accommodated with clean, substantial, well aired habitations, where equal attention hath been paid to rural elegance and conveniency.

Manufacturers and Fisheries

It hath been already observed, that the people here, are particularly attentive to the raising of flax. The reason of this is, that considerable quantities of coarse linen are made every year, which is the only species of manufacture among them, cultivated to any extent. It employs the female hands during winter, and brings a considerable sum into the place. It is bleached and whitened at home, at some small expense. There is an annual market for it in the month of June, where it is bought up by the linen dealers from Glasgow and Paisley, who export the greatest part of the West Indies. Near 7000 yards of cloth, of this coarse fabric are manufactured yearly, which sells at the rate of 1s. to 15d. the yard. At the medium of 13 ½d, the yard, the sum produced, will amount nearly to 389L 11s. 8d.; which sum, divided among the farmers and housekeepers, enables them to pay off their domestic debts with more ease, and punctuality. Another small branch of manufacture is kelp, of which about 10 tons are made up on an average, yearly, and which sells at 3L. the ton. At some former period , a salt-work was carried on upon the shore, that had been employed in the work; but, from some unknown cause, it was given up. Of late, the silk and cotton branches have been introduced, and employ a competent number of hands. From this circumstance, and the attention paid to the making of linen, the number of weavers must greatly exceed that of any other class of mechanicks. Their numbers are, linen weavers 17, cotton 19, silk 3. The other handicraftsmen are, joiners 2, blacksmiths 3, shoemakers 2, tailors 5.

In the districts of the parish, situated upon the shore, fishing was pursued to an extent that ought not to be overlooked in this account. It appears, from the best information that, at the beginning of this century, upwards if 30 boats, belonging to the place, were employed annually in the herring and cod fishery; each boat had 4 men, when at the herring-fishing. From the month of July to October, they were all occupied in this branch. In the months of February and March, about a dozen of these boats, doubly manned, stretched away to the coasts of Galloway, Ireland and Cantire, in search of cod, ling, and oysters. The number of men employed in these fisheries, when in their most flourishing state, could not be less than 150; and the average sum acquired upon them both, might amount to about 600l, Sterling. For many years, however, this trade was on the decline, and the few boats that remained, when depopulation, to be mentioned in the sequel, took place, were in consequence suppressed; since that time no attention has been paid to it, and the art now seems totally lost.

Rent, Farms, &cc.

The real rent of this parish, is 2528L, Sterling. There are about 40 farms in it, which let from 300L. to 36L. There are 19 heritors, or which, 2 of the greater, and 8 of the lesser, are non-resident. The number of sheep is 2000; the most of them are the small black-faced breed. A few of the English breed have been introduced, and are multiplying fast. The wool of the sheep, whose walk is upon the shore, is of a finer quality than that of those who graze upon the hilly grounds, and sells for at least a third more. The sheep upon the higher walks are laid with tar, those upon the lower are not, which perhaps may be one reason of this difference in the pile of the wool. The average quantity of wool fold off the different walks, is about 625 stones yearly. The pasture in this parish, is remarkably favourable for feeding; and both the mutton and beef fattened upon it, upon account of their superior quality in point of flavour and sweetness, have the preference in every market where they are exposed. Of black cattle, there are about 620; Horses 155; of which, within these 12 years the breed is mightily improved. [2]

Population

According to Dr Webster's report, the population in 1755, was 885. From a pretty accurate account lately taken of the number of inhabitants, it appears to amount to 698, young and old. The average number of births, for the last 10 years being 180; of marriages 50; of deaths 100. There is not the smallest doubt that the population of this parish was much greater about 50 years ago, than it is now. The many vestiges of demolished farmhouses to be seen in different places, and the reports of old men, afford sufficient proofs of depopulation. At a medium calculation, there are 100 families fewer now, than formerly; so reckoning at the rate of 6 to a family, makes the number of inhabitants to have decreased from that period, no less than 600. [3]

Ecclesiastical State, Poor, &c.

About 2 years ago, the minister obtained an augmentation to his stipend of 3 chalders of victual, and 20L Scots for communion elements; so the whole living, exclusive of the glebe, which is a very small one, amounts now to 5 chalders of meal, 2 of bear, Linlithgow measure and 420L. Scots; in value, when victual is at a high price, about 126L. Sterling. The Earl of Eglintoune is patron, and titular of the tiends. The manse is but an indifferent one; and though it has received repairs at different times, it is very little mended, but still remains a smoky inconvenient house. It is subjected to a grievance, or, rather a curse which attends most manses, that it stands hard by the village, and part of it projects into the church-yard. The church is built upon a very bad construction. It is a long, narrow, mean looking edifice; low in the walls, and deep roofed. There are few dissenters from the Established Church, in proportion to the number of parishioners; there being about 50 belonging to the 2 common sects of Seceders and Relief, who repair to their several meetings in the neighbouring congregations. – As a proof of the industry, and comfortable situation of the inhabitants, in general, the number of poor is small, there being only 7, at present, upon the pension list of the parish; And, what is much to its credit, there are no wandering beggars belonging to it. There is not an instance in the recollection of anyone living, of a single pauper strolling without the limits of one place. The fund for the maintenance of the poor, is made up mostly from the collections at the church-doors. Of late, it hath received aid from the liberal donations of some generous individuals, to whose bounty, a statistical history, ought to pay the just tribute of encomium.

Antiquities, Remarkable, Occurrences, &c.

This article would afford abundant matter for the antiquary and inquisitive naturalift; but we must abridge as much as possible. We begin with the island of Little Cumbrae. This island is about a mile in length, and half a mile in breadth. It lies in the parallel direction to Bute, from S.W. to N.E. The strata of the rock of which it is composed, are distinctly marked by nature. Viewed at a distance, they seem to lie nearly horizontal; but, upon a nearer approach, they appear to incline to an angle of some elevation. They begin from the water's edge, receding backwards from, and rising one above another to the top, like the steps of a stair. Upon the south side, are a few dwelling-houses, and an old Gothic castle, situated directly opposite to another of the same kind upon the main land. Concerning the antiquity of this castle, nothing can now be learned, and no date or inscription, from which it might be ascertained, has ever been discovered. It seems to have been a place of some strength. It is surrounded by a rampart and a sosse, over which has been a drawbridge. It was surprised and burned by Cromwell's soldiers. The island was then in the possession of the family of Eglintoune, which it has continued to be ever since. In this island, are no fewer than 7 caves. [4]

There are yet to be seen, the ruins of a very ancient chapel, or place of worship, said to have been dedicated to Saint Vey, who lies buried near it; probably, it was a dependency of I. Colm Kill.

Proceeding to the main land, we meet with another old castle called Portencross, directly opposite, as has been observed, to the one upon the Little Isle. Of the history of this, we are able to trace almost as little as the other; but, form its appearance, it bears visible marks of great antiquity. It stands upon rocks to close to the sea, that the waves dash against its defaced walls, and at the very entrance of the inlet or creek that forms the port. It seems to have been a royal hunting seat, one of those places to which the Court retired, to enjoy the diversion of fishing and the chase.[5]

Hitherto, no satisfying account has been given of the origin of the name of this place. In the common language of the country, it is called Pencross, which is just a corruption of its proper ancient name, we may have only conjecture. And, upon a subject to uncertain, we may be allowed to hazard one, just as tenable as any other, in the note below. [6]

The next object of attention in this quarter, is the precipice called Ardneel bank, which lies a little to the northward of Portincross, and forms the promontory or extreme point of land above mentioned. The name is of Gaelic original, and signifies a high point, or Neel's high point. It is truly a noble precipice. A small plain is interjected between it and the water's edge, from which it rises abruptly to the height of more than 230 feet perpendicular. As we approach it upon the South side, we meet with a vast mound of curious heterogeneous matter, which, if there was any vestige of a crater nigh it, one might be ready to pronounce of the volcanic kind. But as there is every reason to conclude, that, not only the plain between the precipice and the water, but the inland valley which runs along the back of it, have once been occupied by the sea, and the precipice itself formed into an island, another theory occurs, namely, that this mound has, at some period, been thrown up by the influx and eddy of the tide, and must have been collecting there for ages; but being at last left dry by the retiring of the sea, through length of time, it is consolidated into a firm compacted mass. As we advance, the rock, composed of different kinds of stone, growns more steep and elevated. At bottom, it is finely skirted with natural shrubbery; farther up, its aged front is adorned with an endless variety of plants, such as hoar-hound, wild thyme, capillus veneris, &c. Toward the summit, it is lined with a thick covering of moss, which gives it a very venerable and grotesque appearance; and here, the whole terminates in 3 distinct cliffs, which, from their exact similarity in figure and altitude, have, time immemorial obtained the appellation of the Three Sisters. In this sequestered scene, where there is so much of the grand and the beautiful, a person given to contemplation, and who loves solitude, may enjoy a walk to great advantage; he will have an opportunity of tracing nature, in some of her more striking features of awfulness and majesty.

This parish, it hath been observed before, abounds with hills; it may indeed be called a system of them. The names of some of them are Gaelic. The most remarkable are, the Tarbet Hill, the Law, the Auld Hill, and the Comb or Camb, which signifies crooked. They have all been used as signal posts in the times of the Danish invasions. By fires from their tops, the alarm was soon given of the appearance of an enemy. Upon the Auld hill, there are the remains of a circular building, which it is likely, was occupied as a watch tower. At the foot of the second, stands another Gothic castle, which takes its name from the hill, the Law, it is one of the completest of the kind to be seen anywhere. It was formerly one of the seats of the Kilmarnock family, who had large possessions in this part of the country; but at what time it was built, no account can be given; but from its appearance, it must be much more modern, than any of the other two already described. The last mentioned hill, is famed for affording fine millstones are in such high repute, as to be demanded from places at the distance of 80 miles; they are dispersed through the Highlands and islands, and some of them exported to Ireland, to America, and the West Indies.

There are no rivers in this parish, but a number of smaller firearms or burns, which, after heavy rains, sometimes come down in vast torrents from the hills. One of these, near the northern boundary of the parish, taking its course through a romantic glen, called the Glen of Southannan, is remarkable for a series of beautiful cataracts, which diminish gradually as the stream approaches the sea. The largest of these falls at the head of the glen, is indeed a striking piece of nature's work. The whole stream issuing with a rapid current from between a high hills, precipitates over a rock from the height of 50 feet, into a deep and awful chasm, the bottom of which, is formed into a capacious sphere, as if it had been hollowed our with a chisel, and resembling a baton tumbled upon its side; over t, the rocks at top, project with threatening majesty. The wildness of the scene is much increased by the fine natural wood that encircles the abyss, where the oak, the hazle, the birch, seem to vie with each other, in displaying their mingled verdure.

Near to this spot, are the ruins of the fine house of Southannan, formerly the residence of the family of Semple, now the property of my Lord Eglintoune. It is built in the Italian taste; a Lord Semple, who resided some time in Italy, in the reign of James the Sixth, brought the model of it from that country. A beautiful green hill, of a secondary order to the Comb, but attached to it, rises with a bold and sudden swell behind the house, from thence we look down upon upon the dismantled fabric of a once splendid dwelling, hiding, as it were, its deformity, among a number of very fine old elms, beeches and ashes, whole venerable boughs, now bending to the earth, bespeak their age; and over the tops of the trees and the ruins, an expanded sheet of water, which at full sea, seems to come in contact with them. Viewed from this point, the landscape is abundantly charming and diversified. A few paces in front, are the remains of a small chapel; the font yet entire.

Eminent Men

Dr. Robert Simpson, late professor of mathematics in the University of Glasgow, whose celebrity in his profession, reflects honour upon the spot that gave him birth, was a native of this place. He long enjoyed a pretty considerable estate in it, which he inherited form his ancestors, but which is now, by purchase, gone out of the family, into the hands of another proprietor. In the obscure retreat, he spent the first years of his life, a period he often recollected with pleasure. At Glasgow, he received the rudiments of that knowledge, which afterward raised him to so much eminence among men of letters. In his Euclid, his Conic-Sections, and other mathematical works, he has left a monument of genius and intellectual ability.
aere perennius
Quod non imber edax, non impotens aquilo
Possit diruere, aut innumerabilis
Annorum feries, et fuga temporum.

Character of the People, Manners, &c.

It may well be accounted a fortunate circumstance for the inhabitants of this place, that their sequestered situation has hitherto secured them from the incroaching influence of that corruption, which in other places of more business and resort, has produced so great a change in the morals of the people. They, on the contrary, have uniformly supported a character for industry, sobriety and decent conduct. The oldest man living, does not recollect an instance of one convicted of a capital crime. Their festive meetings are conducted with much cheerfulness and rural gaiety, but without riot. Their punctuality in paying their debts, at two terms in the year, is now grown into local usage. They are uncommonly regular in their attendance upon public worship; and at church, exhibit a very decent appearance, from the neatness of the dress, and attention to the sacred service. In their behaviour, especially to their superiors, and to strangers, there is an affability and discretion, that distinguishes it remarkably from the morose and sullen rusticity of some of the more inland peasants. In fine, in their labours, their amusements, and the general tenor of their conversation, one may readily recognise the happiness, contentment and comfortable independence, of an honest and peaceable people.

The men are, in their stature, generally above the middle size, stout and well made, and make hardy husbandmen and sailors. And this leads us to observe, that perhaps no country parish in Scotland, has afforded so many men to the sea, as West Kilbride. From a calculation made in the year 1782, it appeared that upwards of 63 men were employed in the service of the Navy, or aboard trading vessels, and some of them were in every action fought at sea, during the late war. At present, the number is considerably less, upon account of the great encouragement, of late years, held out to manufacturers, which induced many young men, who would otherwise have gone to sea, to become weavers; the wages and pay of a seaman, being so much below what can easily be earned by the commonest manufacturer. What a pity is it, that these brave and useful men, from whose toils and dangers, their country acquires so much wealth and glory, are not more adequately rewarded! This change in the inclinations of the young men, which determines them to prefer the manufacturing to the seafaring line, may indeed be more gainful to individuals, but, in a moral view, promises no advantage to the community; as there is some reason to dread, that the ingenious, frank, and manly character of the tar, may, in time, give place to the petulance and effeminacy, the turbulent, factious, and fanatical spirit, which experience has proved to be but too generally attached to people who follow the more domestic occupations.

Concluding Observations

We already took notice, that one capital hinderance to the progress of agricultural improvements, in this part of the country, is the duty on coals; the sepealing of this duty, therefore, will be a most productive mean of promoting those improvements. It will facilitate the procuring of lime, without which, nothing effectual can be done; and when joined to the additional advantage of an excellent road, which the people now enjoy, the great road leading from Greenock to Port-Patrick, puffing through the whole length of the parish, will give a spirit to the exertions of the husbandman hitherto unknown. It will secure the good effect of the example of those more industrious and enterprising farmers, who have already done a great deal, under all the disadvantages of driving lime from a distance. And it will render the more lazy and obstinate ones inexcusable, when every cause of complaint, arising from the great expense of this article shall be removed. [7] This measure may likewise be of great benefit to some proprietors, in another respect, as it will probably induce them to erect salt-works, a branch of manufacture that might be pursued here with profit; as this part of the Frith, being not liable to be affected with freshes from large rivers, the water, from its strong marine impregnation, promises to be productive.

[1] The prejudices of the people are not the only hinderance to the progress of agricultural improvements in this parish. One local disadvantage, which it labours under, must have contributed much to retard them, and that is neither coal nor lime-stone to be found within itself, though pains have been taken to discover them, and attempts made to sink pits for that purpose. And what renders the only expedient, for supplying this defect, more embarrassing is, the duty upon the coals carried coast ways, and even to places within the precincts of the same port, and where the coal works are situated. This hath discouraged farmers form bringing lime-stone by water from Arran, and the greater Cumbray, where it is to be had in abundance, because, though it might be procured from these places,

at no great charge, there is no coal to burn it with, but what must be fetched at an extraordinary expense. The barbarous policy of this law, must appear evident to every person; it hath taken the death of agriculture, wherever its baleful influence hath extended. It must give pleasure to every lover of his country, to observe, that it is now become an object of attention to a virtuous Legislature, who, listening at length to the voice of justice and humanity, have judged it expedient to take it off. In this event, gentlemen, whose estates are situated upon the shore, will be induced to erect straw-kilns. The farmer will have lime afforded him at a moderate rate. A vigorous cultivation will take place. The quantity of grain will be increased and the country assume a new fate.

[2] For some years past, the prices of labour and provisions have been gradually increasing. The wages of an artist have risen from 15d. to 18d. and 22d., and of a common labourer from 1s, to 15d. and 18d. a day. A sheep, which formerly might have been bought for 10s., now brings 16s. and 20s. A lamb cannot be purchased for much below the old price of a sheep. Butter has advanced from 6d. to 9d. and 11d. the pound: And all other articles in proportion. The cause of this rise is easily to be assigned, from the rapid increase of luxury; the different mode of living introduced into every rank; the great demand for hands to be employed in the various branches of manufacturers; and of course the vast influx of people from the country to the great towns, where they immediately find work and good encouragement, which necessarily creates an increasing demand, and a ready market for every article of life.

[3] The reason for this, may be here assigned. About the time above mentioned, some gentlemen of very considerable property in the parish, adopted the idea of grazing, as being better suited to the soil than ploughing, because, from the lightness of it, it naturally runs into grass. In consequence, whole baronies and large tracks of land, formerly planted thick with families, were thrown waste, to make way for this new mode of management; and numbers of these small farms being conjoined, continued to be occupied by one tenant, while the former occupiers ejected from their little possessions, were obliged to remove to other places in quest of bread, and thus carried away from that where they were born, and many of them reared to

manhood, the fruits of their labour and their numbers. We may conceive reasons existing at that time, which might induce proprietors to adopt this practice. The principles of husbandry were not then so well understood; proper attention could not therefore be paid to the land, to work and manage it so as to render it duly productive. The farmers, in those times, had neither the industry nor the enterprising spirit which characterises their successors. There was not the same demand for the produce of a farm, which, at that earlier period, did not bring one-third of the price it does now; consequently, one powerful encouragement to agricultural executions was wanting. The master had his rent paid with less trouble.

But all these reasons taken together, will not compensate the local evils produced by this mode of management: for in the *first* place, it introduced a spirit of engrossing and monopolizing farms, which, as it diminishes the population, has ever been deemed pernicious to the interests of a country. *Secondly,* it enriched a few individuals, at the expense of numbers, who were cast out of bread. *Thirdly*, it gave an immediate check to the progress of agriculture. The old husbandry, even with all its defects was better than none. The object of the monopolizer, being to rear cattle only, he paid little regard to ploughing; of course, the quantity of grain was diminished. The land was neglected and suffered to run into a state of absolute wilderness; so that whole tracks of it are now covered with furze; and, from certain stations, the country presents nothing to the eye, but the bleak appearance of a forest. The consequence, upon the whole, has been, that when, in other places, farming, in its present improved forms, had made considerable advances, in this parish it had made none. In the *last* place, as has been observed before, it gave the finishing hand to the destruction of the fishery. Gentlemen it would appear, are now sensible to these evils, at least, in as far as the interests of agriculture have been affected by them; and it seems to be their wish to have their estates re-peopled , and they have put their tenants upon such a footing, by the late leases, as to make it their interest to clear and cultivate the land; from which the most beneficial effects may be expected.

[4] Two of them only are very remarkable. One of these, is a square room of 31 feet, so high in the roof, that a person may stand upright, and seems to be the work of art. The other, which is the largest of the whole, penetrates so far, as never yet to have been explored. The certainty of meeting with dams and roepheitick air, renders such an attempt dangerous, if not impracticable. Concerning the use of these caves, tradition conveys nothing certain, and the legendary tales of superstition respecting them, are too ridiculous to deserve notice.

[5] What leads to this conjecture, is, that there is full extant in the possession of Robert Hunter, Esq. of Hunterston, a charter of seasin, signed by Robert the Second at this castle, in the 1374, being the 4th year of his reign, vesting the family of Hunterston, in the property of certain parts of the lands of Ardneel; and to which deed, the names of several nobles who attended the King in that excursion, and composed part of his court, are appended as witnesses.

[6] The promontory, near to which, this port and castle are situated, is the extreme point of land directly West from Edinburgh. To this day, the track on a line of road, can be distinctly traced through the country, leading from the capital to this port. From this circumstance, as well as from the very name, we conclude it must have been a place of some consequence. In these barbarous and remote times, there could be no trade carried on in it, to give it that consequence. Neither can it be imagined, there was so much communication between the Highlands and the main land, as that this place might be converted into a mere ferry port, for the convenience of passengers, who we may believe, would hardly be induced, either from profit or curiosity, to visit these inhospitable regions.

The most probable account, therefore of the matter, seems to be that this was the place where they took boat to go over to the celebrated monastery of I. Colm Kill, the most ancient foundation of the kind in Scotland, and which, it is well known, was, for many ages, the burial place of our Scottish Kings. And, as this monastery was established long before any other in this country, it may be supposed, that, in that period of the gloomy reign of superstition, many pilgrimages were made to it. Hence, the name Portincross, being composed of

Portus and Crucis; from this port, was the nearest and most direct passage over to the royal cemetery, and from it too, the pious travellers took their departure to do penance, or make their offerings at the sacred place. What corroborates this conjecture somewhat, is, that at Lochransa in the North end of the Arran, there is an old castle, where tradition reports, the companies passing to the western isles (whether these funeral and pilgrimage processions, is uncertain), were wont to stop and refresh; and then, as may be concluded, crossing over the narrow Isthmus of Cantire, and again taking boat, after sailing through the sound between Islay and Jura, were immediately at Iona, the object of their destination. This port and castle have become full more remarkable, from an occurrence that happened near them, and which deserves to be taken notice of here, namely the loss of one of the Spanish ships, that composed the famous Armada, intended for the conquest of England, in the year 1588, in consequence of their dispersion by a storm after the action with the English fleet. She sunk in about 10 fathom water, at no great distance from the shore. It is difficult to assign a reason for the accident; the probability is, that coming up the Frith, with easy weather, and all sail up, and ports open, a sudden gust from the land, which often happens in narrow seas, had overset her. An attempt was made some more than 50 years ago, by means of a diving machine, to examine her situation, and whether it was possible to weigh her, or to recover what was most valuable belonging to her. The diver reported that from the size of her guns, she appeared to be a capital ship; and a very large chest was perceived fixed upon deck. The operation succeeded so far, that some fine brass guns were brought up, and a smaller iron one, which still lies on the beach. This piece of ordnance, has undergone many inspection, and various opinions have been formed about the weight of its shot. To judge form the calibre of it, in its present corroded state, it seems to have been a 14 or 16 pounder. A second attempt was to have been made, with a new and more complete apparatus, when, it is probable, much more of the wreck would have been recovered, but the death of one of the undertakers unfortunately put an end to the scheme.

Within the very same place where the Spanish ship went down, a fine vessel belonging to Glasgow, the richest that ever was fitted out from this country, and the property of Glasford and Company, was also lost, in the spring of the year 1770. This disaster was occasioned, not by the stress of weather, but through the inadvertency of the ship's company, in allowing the vessel to drift too far in during the night, ere the lighthouse was perceived, and in endeavouring to put her about, the masted stays, and went upon the rocks.

[7] Another thing of great importance to be attended to is, the reviving and restoring the fisheries. As farming and fishing cannot conveniently and effectually be carried on together, the last ought to be put upon such a footing, and such encouragement given, as to render it worth any person's while to pursue it as a separate branch. In order to this, as it is absolutely requisite to have some proper station, to which boats may have easy access upon all occasions and may lie in safety; and also proper habitations for the accommodation of the fishers and their families. Upon a bleak and open coast, such as this, and where there is so much foul ground, a stable and regular fishing can never take place without these provisions. Hitherto, this shore has afforded nothing of the kind. The port of Portincross does not answer the purpose, the entrance of it is so environed with rocks, that boats can only take it in easy weather, and they must be drawn up without the reach of an impetuous surge which drives in with every gale. A little to the northward of the old port, between it, and a place called the Throughlet, the entrance to the precipice above decribed, nature points out a spot, which by the hand of the art and industry, might be formed into an excellent fishing station. There is a fine natural inlet, upon which there is always sufficient depth of water, and which could be easily widened to the design; within, a spacious bason might be scooped out, where boats and smacks of all dimensions might enter and lie in the most perfect security in all weathers. Around this place, is a great deal of barren land, which at present yields but indifferent pasture. This might be profitably laid out in steadings and gardens for the convenience of those employed in the fishing. The execution of this scheme, no doubt, would be attended with considerable expense; bit if it is practicable, what can men of property do with their money that is better? are they not to be blamed for neglecting undertakings, where they might lay it out with advantage, and do essential service to their country?

If fishing was considered as an object, 80 years ago, when the price of fish of all kinds was low; and even under all the disadvantages arising from the want of a convenient harbour: much more would it be an object now, when the prices are advanced in a four, fix, and tenfold proportion, and when every encouragement was given that the nature of the business requires.

Notes: Civic Society Thanks

Note: This was a note placed on the Facebook group to thank the Civic Society. It is appropriate to repeat it here, as without their permission the group would have been much less interesting.

Glad to inform the Group that the West Kilbride Civic Society (successors to the Amenity Society) have given their permission for their works to be shared by us, so long as it is attributed. This means that I will be able to post pages of their rare books that are now extremely hard and expensive to come by. So, a big thanks to them.

A History of West Kilbride in 100 Objects: Portencross Prince

Mrs G.V. Blair, when she was young, enjoyed nothing more than a stay at the seaside town of West Kilbride, and a trip to Portencross. Later in life, she and her husband enjoyed breeding champion dogs. On April 4th, 1933, a baby Dalmatian was born to father Golden Arrow and mother Queen Rubalex. The baby dog was named PORTENCROSS PRINCE.

Portencross Prince became a celebrated champion Dalmatian during the 1930's in both Scotland and England. He went on to win an incredible 10 challenge certificates including 1935 Blackpool, Harrogate, Edinburgh; 1936 Glasgow, British Dalmatian Club, Belfast and Crystal Palace; 1937 Glasgow, Crufts and the British Dalmation Club.

The Champion also won the British Dalmation Club Best in Show Award two years in a row - 1936 and 1937. Shown below is the cigarette card issued in 1938 in his honour.

Ch. Portencross Prince

CHAMPION
DOGS
A SERIES OF REAL PHOTOS
No. 22

DALMATIAN.
CH. PORTENCROSS PRINCE.

Sire : Golden Arrow. *Dam :* Queen Rubalex. *Born :* April 4th, 1933.

Winner of 10 Challenge Certificates, including : 1935 : Blackpool ; Harrogate ; Edinburgh. 1936 : Glasgow ; British Dalmatian Club ; Belfast ; Crystal Palace. 1937 : Glasgow ; Cruft's ; British Dalmatian Club. Best in Show, Dalmatian Club, 1936 and 1937.

Owned by : Mrs. G. V. Blair, 12, Queen's Gate, Glasgow.

ISSUED BY

JOHN SINCLAIR LTD
NEWCASTLE-ON-TYNE

Derivation of Place Names: Springside House / Hyndman Road

The Springside estate sits below Law Hill on the North West "Corner". The house sits on the edge of what was anciently called "The Orchard" below Law Castle, and Orchard House (photo to come one day soon). Below Springside and The Orchard was St Cuthbert's Wood (Cubrieshaw) - the remnants of which can still be seen today in the trees that continue to grow all around Law Brae.

It is only natural that a spring would develop from water running down Law Hill and so we can probably guess that the estate sits upon a natural spring. I have attached an old postcard of Springside House herewith (c. 1906).

In the 17th and 18th Century, Springside was the home of the Hyndman family, from whom we get Hyndman Road in Seamill.

Derivation of Place Names: Kirkcroft

This piece of land now sits under the Wellington Hotel, and was formerly the site of the religious day markets – such as St. Brigids day on 1st February and St. Colm's (Columba's) day. The original word "Croft", in the Scots language, means "a land of superior quality kept constantly manured, and under crop, smallholding" 9. So the Kirkcroft would have been the farm belonging to the church. This was certainly true in the late medieval period when the church owned the most fertile land in the village and particularly the stretch of land from the Kirk Croft to the foot of Drummilling Hill. The market stretched over to the wall of the Barony.

In the week prior to market day, the cattle, pigs etc. were brought in from the fields along the drovers route now a footpath alongside the Community Centre, down Half way street and into the holding pen which would have been the small triangle of grass land still the "Village Green" beside the library.

This practice was fairly common in Scotland and if you visit any other small villages, look for the old local Dairy as it may well sit opposite the "Village Green".

The pigs and cattle would then be taken one at a time into the back of the old dairy for slaughtering ready for market on Kirkcroft.

History: Village View Newspaper

In 1978, as a 15 year old, I and my friend Scott Brady (now Scott Brady Q.C. of the Middle Temple) decided to establish a monthly village newspaper entitled Village View. He was the real writing skill in the paper which he called a "paragon of literary virtue", whereas I was more the poor schlep that had to try to get everyone on board wth the idea. As a result I was co-opted onto the Community Council under Colonel Maclean's Chairmanship alongside the legendary Mae Kellock and Cllr Edith Clarkson who were all incredibly encouraging.

The paper basically had any news and views from around the village. It contained news of houses for sale- kindly supplied, and sponsored by Lindsay Wilkie Ltd (his brother ran the West Kilbride office and was a lovely man). The price was 10p and the circulation reached the steady heights of 400 copies. Scott largely wrote the stories although I occasionally got involved as a junior reporter. i remember I got to "interview" Scott Grier when he received his MBE. Total revenue was £40 therefore plus about £10 - £20 in advertising revenue - which all went into the coffers of the Community Council as they paid for the paper and copying.

Occasionally, when it was a slow news month, we would write letters to the paper ourselves to fill space, as I recall. As young lads, we thought we had full editorial control, but Mae Kellock was the final word! After a year, Scott went off to university and I ran the paper for a year after that. Then it was my turn to go up to Glasgow and although I tried for a few months to keep it going, it finally bit the dust in 1980.

Some years later, Charlie Garratt and Peter Fry established the Village Voice (I still have some of the copies). I was consulted about the project and I did offer to help, but I think they had already decided a way forward without the need for my assistance. It was a huge success for a while until, if I remember correctly, the work to print and collate the magazine became so heavy or costly a burden, it closed.

Perhaps this Facebook Page offers us much, much more than either of these papers ever could and it is such a pleasure for me to be involved again.

Transcripts: 'The Topographical, Statistical, and Historical Gazetteer of Scotland' (1848)

KILBRIDE (West), a parish on the coast of the district of Cunningham, Ayrshire; bounded on the north by Largs; on the east by Dalry; on the south-east by Ardrossan; and on all other sides by the frith of Clyde. It occupies the angle formed by the recession of the coast-line on the opening or commencement of the expansive bay of Ayr on the north; and presenting one side to that bay, another to the strait or sound between the coast and the Cumbrays, and a third to the interior, is nearly of a triangular figure. Its extreme length from north to south is about 6 miles; and its extreme breadth from the promontory of Portincross eastward is about 3 miles. The island of Little Cumbray is attached to the parish; but, having been separately noticed in the article Cumbraes, it needs not here be kept in view. A continuation of the rolling surface of hill and upland which commences at Greenock, and forms a sea-screen down the coast of Renfrewshire, comes boldly in upon the parish, especially on its eastern verge, and undulates over its whole area, softening in character as it approaches the south. Along the eastern frontier, the hills run so regularly and loftily in a ridge as to form a natural boundary, and send up one summit—that of Kame—nearly 1,000 feet above sea-level. In the interior, as they deflect to the west, they are in some instances concatenated, and in others insulated; and, in general, they decline in height as they approach the frith. The hills are, in many instances, green to their summits; and, regarded as a field of heights, are ploughed by various romantic little vales, bringing down their watery tributes to the sea, and are occasionally made the screen or protecting framework of luxuriantly tinted haughs. From the summits of many of them views are obtained, in peculiarly advantageous grouping, of that magnificent landscape of far-stretching lowland-coast, luscious in the beauties of cultivation, and long expanse of bright blue sea, romantic in its islands and its land-locking boundaries, and background scenery of Highland heights, of soaring and pinnacled mountain elevations, which is descried from great multitudes of the rising grounds of Ayrshire, and the stirring and arousing appeals of which might have been expected to produce more than one 'Ayrshire bard,' and to have provoked that one to the breathing of more warmth of colouring over his efforts at description. "At one view," says the sufficiently unexcited writer in the Old Statistical Account, "the eye takes in the broken land and small sounds formed by the islands of Arran, Bute, the two Cumbrays, and the coasts of Cowal and Cantire; the extensive coast of Carrick, from Ayr to Ballentrae; a wide expanded frith, with the rock of Ailsa rising majestic in its very bosom; the stupendous rocks and peak of Goatfield in Arran; while the distant cliffs of Jura are seen just peeping over the whole, in the back ground. Such a landscape is exceedingly rare, and has always been particularly pleasing to strangers." Five rills or burns, with their tiny tributaries, all begin and end their course within the limits of the parish, and are the only streams by which it is watered, but, in rainy weather, they sometimes come down in a bulk of volume and power of current which invest them with importance. Kilbride - burn, the largest of them, rises on the west side of Glenton-hill, flows past the village of West Kilbride, and enters the frith at Sea-Mill. South Annan-burn, near the northern boundary, pursues its course through a romantic glen, and forms a series of beautiful cataracts, diminishing in depth of leap as the brook approaches the sea. At the highest and principal fall, the burn, emerging with a rapid current from between two high hills, leaps right over a rocky precipice 50 feet in height, into a deep and awful chasm, the bottom of which is a capacious sphere, smooth and regular as if hollowed out with the chisel. Over the abyss project the beetling and menacing rocks of the precipice; and around it are a zone and tuftings of natural wood, in which the oak, the hazel, and the birch vie for the pre-eminence of shade and verdure. The coast-line of the parish, owing to the advantage gained by peninsularity of form, is about 7 miles in extent. At the angle, or south-west extremity, projects the promontory of Portincross, terminating in a perpendicular wall of rock 300 feet high, called Ardneil bank, or Goldberry-head, separated from the margin of the sea only by a very narrow belt of verdant land, and extending in a straight line of about a mile in length. Natural wood, consisting of oak, hazel, ash, and hawthorn, runs in thick tuftings along the base of the precipice, and ivy, with gray and golden coloured lichens, impresses a beautiful tracery of tint and of aspect athwart its bold front. To approach the terrific summit makes even a man of firm nerve giddy; but to view it from below is to enjoy a rich feasting of the taste and the fancy. Everywhere, except at this remarkable headland, the coast of the parish is low and shelving. From the northern boundary to a point about two miles south, stretch the sands of South Annan, of half-moon form, sheltered by a curving recess in the land, measuring at their centre, when the tide is out, about a mile in breadth, rich in their beds of mussels, cockles, and other shell-fish, and offering a favourite retreat to vast flocks of various kinds of wild fowl. Limestone occurs at Ardneil, and in some other localities, but too scantily and of too poor a quality to be profitably worked. On a conspicuous hill, called the Law, are quarried millstones of a coarse sort of granite. The soil over nearly four-fifths of the whole area, or up the sides and over the summits of its almost incessant heights, is poor, mossy, and moorland, on a subsoil of coarse till, yet admitting, around the bases and on the lower sides of the heights, not a few patches of loamy and calcareous land of kindly and fertile character. About two-thirds, or a little more, of the entire area is regularly or occasionally subjected to the plough; and nearly one-third is naturally and exclusively pastoral. The district is characteristically devoted to the dairy, the arable pastures being used and esteemed for their produce in Dunlop cheese. The parish is, in general, sufficiently enclosed; but, with some small exceptions, it is destitute of plantation, and has a naked and chilled appearance. At Portincross is a small quay, offering accommodation at high water to vessels of 40 or 50 tons burden, and used in making shipments for the Clyde. The road from Greenock to Ardrossan runs along the parish, and, along with subordinate roads, gives it an aggregate length of 22 miles broad, — preserved in good repair, and suitably provided with bridges. Population, in 1801, 795; in 1831, 1,685. Houses 215. Assessed property, in 1815, £7,006.

On a ledge of rock, close upon the sea, under the bold promontory of Ardneil bank, stand the ruinous yet tolerably complete walls of the very ancient castle of Portincross. The promontory being, with the exception of the Rhinns of Galloway, the extreme western point of the Lowlands of Scotland, and lying conveniently between Edinburgh and Icolmkill, and also between Dundonald and Rothsay, the castle was probably a halting-place of the Scottish kings on embarking either for Bute or for the burying-place of their early ancestors. Some charters of the first and the second Stuarts purport to have received the sign-manual at "Arnele," and may possibly evince this castle—however small and incommodious—to have worn, in a limited degree, similar honours to those of the homogeneous castle of Dundonald: see DUNDONALD. A brief distance seaward from the promontory, at a spot where the depth of water is 10 fathoms, sunk a principal ship of the famous Spanish armada. Of several pieces of ordnance which, about a century ago, were brought up from her by means of a diving machine, one lies in a corroded state on the shore beside the old castle. — The most remarkable of the hills of the parish, especially those called Tarbet-hill, the Law, Auld-hill, and the Comb, or Caimb, or Kaim, were all used as signal-posts, or the arenæ of beacon-fires, during the period of the Danish invasions. On Auld-hill, are remains of a circular building, which probably was occupied as a watch-tower. On the Law, overlooking the village, are the ruinous walls of Law-castle, a stately and very ancient tower, formerly one of the seats of the Earls of Kilmarnock. - Near the fine cascade of South Annan-burn, stand the ruins of a very elegant mansion, formerly the residence of the family of Semple, and now the property of the Earl of Eglinton. The house was built in the reign of James VI. by a Lord Semple, who brought the model of it from Italy. A beautiful green hill, secondary to the Kaim, but attached to it, rises with a bold and sudden swell behind the house. Standing on its summit, a spectator looks down upon the dismantled fabric of the once-elegant mansion, hiding, as it were, the scathings of its beauty among a number of very fine old elms, beeches, and ashes, whose venerable boughs now bending to the earth indicate their age; and over the tops of the trees and the ruin, he looks abroad on an expanded sheet of water which, at full sea, seems to come in contact with them, and on an abundantly charming and finely diversified grouping of that vast and gorgeous landscape, which is seen from most of the heights of the parish, — but nowhere with more advantage of fore-ground and of general effect than from this eminence. Immediately adjoining the ruin of the Semple mansion, stands a neat modern cottage ornée. Near the coast, about 1 or 1½ mile south of Southennan, in a position which originally was a narrow and small peninsula running into a morass, stands the ancient mansion of Hunterston, now occupied as a farm-house, and sending up a square tower of apparently high antiquity. The modern mansion, a handsome new edifice, is nearer the sea. — Dr. Robert Simson, the well-known professor of mathematics in the University of Glasgow a7id the translator and editor of Euclid, and General Robert Boyd, Lieutenant-governor of Gibraltar during the notable siege of that great fort in 1782, were natives of the parish. The village of West Kilbride is situated in a well-sheltered hollow, ¾ of a mile from the sea ; 1¾ mile from Portincross-castle ; 4½ miles north-west from Ardrossan; and 7¼ miles south from Largs. On the streamlet which runs through it are two mills for grinding oats, a flax-mill, a mill for grinding tanners' bark, and a mill for pulverizing charcoal. A tannery employs 8 or 10 persons. The chief employments are weaving and hand-sewing in subordination to the manufacturers of Glasgow and Paisley. In 1838, 85 harness-looms and 5 plain looms were employed on fabrics in all the three departments of cotton, silk, and woollen. The condition of the weavers, as in most other places, is painfully depressed. Near the centre of the village, on a gentle rising ground, stands the parish-church, a long narrow mean-looking edifice, low in the walls and deep-roofed. A meeting-house belonging to the United Secession, is a neat and commodious structure. In the village are three schools, one of them parochial, and the others private, and unendowed; a library, containing upwards of 400 volumes; and three Friendly societies, — one of them of considerably long standing. Population of the village, about 1,020. — West Kilbride is in the presbytery of Irvine, and synod of Glasgow and Ayr. Patron, the Earl of Eglinton. Stipend £202 12s. 7d.; glebe £13 12s. 7d. Unappropriated teinds £383 18s. 2d. Parochial schoolmaster's salary £27 17s. 8d., with £37 6s. 9d. fees. - The saint from whom the parish, like the other

Kilbrides of Scotland, has its name, is the well-known Bridget, familiarly called Bride. The church anciently belonged to the monks of Kilwinning, and was served by a vicar. In the parish there were, previous to the Reformation, several chapels. One stood on the coast, 1¼ mile south of the church, at a place to which it gave the name of Chapelton. Another stood at Southennan, in the immediate vicinity of the ancient mansion of the family of Sempell; and was built by John, Lord Sempil, in the reign of James IV., and dedicated to Saint Inan, - reported to have been a confessor at Irvine, and to have died in the year 839. A third, subordinate like the others to the parish-church, was dedicated to Saint Bege or Veg, said to have been a Scottish virgin and confessor, who died in 896, and situated in Little Cumbray.

Notes: Latest Views (11th November)

Note. The Facebook group was established at the end of October 2015, and before two weeks had elapsed 1,500 people had joined and many, many were active. This was an incredibly humbling experience and one that I certainly had not expected. I therefore penned the following statement. After posting the statement, I received so many encouraging comments from around the world. Therefore the "history" of the Facebook group would seem to be incomplete without this.

Thanks so much to everyone that has sent me glad tidings in this last crazy week. I have had messages of support from the four corners of the globe - from many old friends and even more new. I am only sorry I have been unable to spend as much time with each and every one of you as I would like, but I think that will come in due course. I do have other responsibilities here on the West Coast, and whilst I am in the enviable position of being able to make my own hours to some degree, there are others who do rely upon me. I am hopeful that you will understand, and that together we can make this excellent group something for the long term, and for all generations who have any connection with our beloved village, however tenuous.

You will have gathered that I am only just beginning to realise some of the potential here to bring a lot of joy to a lot of people in the form of history, heritage and memories of our home. I am not simply trying to fire as much up on Facebook as possible, but I am trying to build archives in the Albums section and the Files Section (maybe one day in the video's section hahahaha), so that going forward you, your kith and kin, and even your descendants will be able to go back in time and view West Kilbride from all angles. Sure some of our history is not as appealing as we might like it to be, but warts and all, we are who we are - and clearly that is something to be extremely proud of.

For me, the most exciting thing has been the dialogue, the shared memories, the enthusiasm to share photos and stories, with a common and joyous regard to the goodwill of people we might never ever meet, yet accepted as brothers and sisters across so many other divides - geographic, temporal, or whatever "end" of the village you came from. Being West Kilbride for me has smashed those divides, perceived or real and brought us back to a fantastic sense of community that I definitely know you share with me. I am sorry that I have not yet had time to take on board everyone's ideas. I am particularly excited about the young people that have contacted me with a burning interest in what we are doing here, and of course the contact with the local school. The notion of adding heritage tourism to supplement the already fantastic work done by the West Kilbride Community Initiative in the form of Craft Town Scotland, excites me and gives us a trajectory that establishes yet another purpose for our endeavours here.

So we press on. My wife and others have said I need to pace things a little better. I do have a lot more I want to share with you, and I fully intend to do that. I wanted to get a reasonable amount of content up quickly to show you some of the potential we can make together. I love every single minute of this, and I am learning about Facebook as I go along.

They way I do things may change to make it more efficient, but we shall journey in that together. Please do feel free to invite as many friends as you like, share as many memories, and participate in any discussions. I only ask that you maintain a respectful dialogue, be tolerant of the views of others, and remember that all ages use this Facebook Group. In our history, we have been plagued by division, I would not like that to happen in any way here.

So, I intend to crack on, more in the sense of a pop in pop out, add more things as we go sense, and try and use my over active imagination to stimulate conversations about "Being West Kilbride". Please make a regular point of visiting the albums and the documents sections of the Group, as I will be trying to add as much as I can there to provide an archive of material that you can enjoy, share and discuss as much as you want.

Meantime, I would thank you all again sooooooo much for making this soooooo easy, and for being so warm and kind over my tiny efforts. I hope that you will continue to enjoy this for a great long time to come, and West Kilbride (you know who you are), I am and will always remain, your humble and obedient servant.

A History of West Kilbride in 100 Objects: The Bridgend Mural

Auchenames is an ancient Barony in Portencross (Portincross), stretching back to the 1320 when the lands were granted to Reginald Crawfurd of Crosbie. In the late middle ages the estate of Crosbie became the junior branch, leaving Auchenames, but then in the late 16th century it was returned to the estate through marriage of Jean Crawfurd back into her own distant Crawfurd family.

The Bridgend Mural stating "I.C." "Maii" and "1623"

In 1623, Jean Crawfurd ordered the building of the bridge across the West Kilbride burn, connecting Cubrieshaw (St Cuthbert's wood) and the main street. The builders stone on the bridge remains to this day.

For more details on the medieval Auchinames and Crosbie families, see the entry on Portincross.

The last internally recognised chief was Hugh Ronald George Craufurd, who sold his land (Auchenames, Crosbie and other estates) and moved to Canada in 1904. He died in Calgary in 1942, leaving no male heirs.

Derivation of Place Names: Halfway Street / Happy Hills

Half Way Street is marked on several old maps as the "Haef Weg" or "Haaf Weg". This is old Norse (Viking) for "Sea Way". It is a traditional public right of way through the village, over the top of Corsehill ("Crosbie Hill") right down to the sea at Portencross (see the map attached from 1827 showing Half Way as the road that reaches Portencross Castle. This is because the extension of "Portencross Road" down the hill to the crossroads was originally called "Crosshill Road" - I will be showing a postcard of this sometime (once again "Crosbie Hill) but a newer road than the original.

We can only guess how viking language came to our village. In the battle of Largs of 1263, apparently the skirmish that lasted on Goldenberry Hill was strategically important for the outcome. The Craufurds of Crosbie were the leaders of that battle.

Happy Hills simply derives its name from "Haef Weg" and would actually have been "Haef Weg Hills" but who could pronounce that?

Derivation of Place Names: Drummilling

Drummilling, prior to the building of the estate of houses, was the location of two 17th century farmsteads. These are marked on the 1604 map drawn up by the Reverend Pont in his travels around Scotland.

Isaac Jackson believed that the name came from the Gaelic "Drum" meaning "height" and the middle English "mylen" being "mill" making the "high mill". Other commentators have regarded the name as "the height of sweet feeding"

However, old Scots has the derivative of the word mailing (e.g. Thirdmailing) as an agricultural property that is rented

In 1390 we have a text from old Scots:

"The qwhilk tounis the forsaid Sir J. has in *malyng* of Jonet Gourlay"

In 1527 in Selkirk another document:

"I ... to have set and to *maling* latting ... ten merkis vorcht of land"

We are therefore left with the fairly reasonable conclusion that Drummilling means the "high farmstead".

History: Robert Simson

Born: 14 October 1687 in West Kilbride,

Died: 1 October 1768 in Glasgow, Scotland

Robert Simson was the eldest son of John Simson and Agnes Simson (née Simson). Simson's mother had 17 children, all boys, only six of whom reached manhood. Simson entered the University of Glasgow as a student on 3 March 1702, being 14 years old at the time, and studied under the regent John Tran. He distinguished himself in classics, oriental languages and botany.

His father had intended that Robert should enter the church, and it was only by accident that his interests turned to mathematics. As a student of theology he was required to produce written work for his teachers. This he found unsatisfying, since he felt the arguments to be inconclusive and speculative. For recreation he turned first to a book on oriental philology, where he found statements that could be shown to be true or false, but this was not wholly satisfying and at that stage he had recourse to mathematics and Euclid's *Elements.* He then set to work to study mathematics seriously, but he had to do this on his own, since at that time, for some reason, there were no lectures given on the subject by the professor Robert Sinclair.

ROBERTUS SIMSON, M. D.
MATHESEOS IN ACADEMIA GLASGUENSI
PROFESSOR
Obiit ipsis Kalendis Octobris Anno 1768

During his first year as a student in Glasgow Robert Simson was involved in a rather interesting incident, which shows that, even before the Union of the Parliaments, Scottish as well as English students celebrated the 5th of November with fireworks. On emerging from a close that night Robert was hurt in the face by shot from a pistol belonging to a fellow student Arthur Tran, who with a group of other students was firing a pistol and letting off squibs. They were hauled before the Faculty where Tran agreed that he had fired the pistol, and that he had said *he would shoot it in some old wife's lug.*

Tran himself was fined half-a-crown, his friends lesser amounts and were publicly rebuked in the Common Hall. Tran may have been the son of the regent John Tran.

It is generally supposed that Robert Simson attended the University as a student for a period of about eight years until 1710, this was not an unusual period of study at the time. In 1710 Professor Robert Sinclair resigned, and Simson was offered the chair. He was disinclined to accept it immediately, and asked permission to spend some time in London, where he might have the opportunity to become acquainted with some of the most eminent mathematicians in England. This was granted and he went immediately to London where he met several well-known mathematicians, such as Edmond Halley, John Caswell (d. 1712), Savilian Professor of Geometry at Oxford, William Jones, and finally Humphrey Ditton (1675-1715), Mathematical Master at Christ's Hospital, with whom Simson was particularly friendly. While in London he was informed that, by the Faculty minute of 8 March 1711, he had been nominated to the Glasgow chair

providing always, that he gives a satisfactory proof to the faculty of his skill in the Mathematics before his admission.

He returned to Glasgow, where on 10 November 1711 he was given two geometrical problems to resolve. These he dealt with to the satisfaction of the Faculty

after which he gave a satisfactory specimen of his skill in mathematicks and dexterity in teaching geometry and algebra, he also produced sufficient testimonials from Mr Caswell the Professor of astronomy at Oxford and from others in London well skilled in the mathematicks, upon all which the faculty resolve he shall be admitted the nineteenth day of this instant November.

Three days before his admission he graduated Master of Arts.
It was while he was in England that Edmond Halley suggested to him that he might devote his considerable talents to the restoration of

the work of the early Greek geometers, such as Euclid and Apollonius of Perga. These are works that only survive in abbreviated accounts given by later mathematicians such as Pappus of Alexandria. He first studied Euclid's so-called porisms. Playfair's 1792 definition of porism is

a proposition affirming the possibility of finding such conditions as will render a certain problem indeterminate, or capable of innumerable solutions.

Simson's work on Euclid's porisms was published in 1723 in the *Philosophical Transactions of the Royal Society,* and his restoration of the *Loci Plani* of Apollonius appeared in 1749. Further work of his on porisms and other subjects including logarithms was published posthumously in 1776 by Lord Stanhope at his own expense. Simson also set himself the task of preparing an edition of Euclid's *Elements* in as perfect a form as possible, and his edition of Euclid's books 1-6, 11 and 12 was for many years the standard text and formed the basis of textbooks on geometry written by other authors. The work ran through more than 70 different editions, revisions or translations published first in Glasgow in 1756, with others appearing in Glasgow, Edinburgh, Dublin, London, Cambridge, Paris and a number of other European and American cities. Recent editions appeared in London and Toronto in 1933 under the editorship of Isaac Todhunter, and in São Paolo in 1944. Simson's lectures were delivered in Latin, at any rate at the beginning of his career. His most important writings were written in that language, however, his edition of Euclid, after its first publication in Latin, appeared in English, as did a treatise on conic sections that he wrote for the benefit of his students.

His reputation as a geometer has always been very high, although, as a critic wrote

the additions and alterations which Simson made by way of restoring the text to its 'original accuracy' are certainly not all of them improvements, and the notes he appended show with what reverence he regarded the great geometers of antiquity.

There was a feeling in some quarters that, by limiting his efforts to the attainment of he perfect text, he lost an opportunity of applying his own considerable talents and insight to a more useful exposition of his subject. For Simson the best vehicle for presenting a mathematical argument was geometry and, although he was familiar with the recent developments in algebra and the infinitesimal calculus, he preferred to express himself in geometrical terms wherever possible. He was not, of course, alone in this, as Newton had adopted the same viewpoint when writing his *Principia*.

That Simson's work was not restricted to Greek geometry is illustrated by Tweddle's paper, in which he discusses an early manuscript of Simson dealing with inverse tangent series and their use in calculating π.

For fifty years Simson lectured five days a week during term time to his two main classes. By all accounts he was a good lecturer, although better in his younger days than towards the end of his life, when his absence of mind made him the victim of practical jokes. Several of his pupils achieved distinction in mathematics, notably Maclaurin, Stewart, John Robison who became Professor of Natural Philosophy in the University of Edinburgh and Trail.
Simson was a good looking man, tall of stature and favouring light coloured cloths. He was unmarried and so had no use of the commodious house in the College to which he was entitled, but lived in rooms there. He ate all his meals, including breakfast, at a small tavern opposite the College gate kept by a Mrs Millar. He delighted in showing visitors round the College and was very knowledgeable about the large collection of Roman antiquities coming from the Antonine Wall and its neighbourhood.

According to the Reverend Alexander Carlyle

He was particularly averse to the company of ladies, and, except one day in the year, when he drank tea at Principal Campbell's and conversed with gaiety and ease with his daughter Mally, who was always his first toast, he was never in company with them. It is said to have been otherwise with him in his youth, and that he had been much attached to one lady, to whom he had made proposals, but on

*her refusing him he became disgusted with the sex. The lady was
dead before I became acquainted with the family, but her husband I
knew, and must confess that in her choice the lady preferred a satyr
to Hyperion.*

Simson was a sociable man. On Friday evenings he would meet with
friends at a club in a nearby tavern, where he would play whist, a
game in which he excelled. This was followed by a period of
conversation and singing. He was fond of singing Greek odes set to
contemporary music.

Every Saturday he would walk, alone or in company, to an inn in the
nearby village of Anderston, where he played host to his particular
friends and any visitors to Glasgow that he had invited to join him
for dinner.

He was a most methodical man and, on daily walks in the College
garden and elsewhere, he counted the number of paces from one
place to another.

Robert Simson was the first person to be appointed to the office of
Clerk (later known as Clerk of Senate), which he took up in 1728
and only demitted when he retired in 1761. In 1761 he retired from
his chair having held it for fifty years. He kept his rooms in the
tower until his death, but gave up his College house, which he had
never lived in. Simson remained in good health until a few years
before his death, during which period he had to employ an
amanuensis to assist him in revising his geometrical writings.

A year before he retired from the Chair of Mathematics, Simson had
proposed that his colleague James Buchanan, the Professor of
Oriental Languages, should relieve him of his teaching duties on
condition of succeeding to the Chair when he retired, but Buchanan
died before any action was taken. Before Simson retired in 1761 he
stipulated that his Assistant James Williamson should succeed him,
and this was agreed.

Robert Simson died in his eighty-first year and was buried in the
neighbouring Blackfriars burial ground, where a marble tombstone,

bearing a long laudatory Latin inscription, was raised in his memory. Later, through the efforts of a Mr Fullerton of Overton in the parish of West Kilbride, an imposing monument fifty feet high was erected in West Kilbride cemetery, bearing the inscription in which he is described as

the Restorer of Grecian Geometry, and by his Works the Great Promoter of its Study in the Schools.

Simson bequeathed his very large library of books and papers to the University of Glasgow, where they comprise the valuable Simson Bequest. The collection includes the sixteen volumes of his daily notebooks, the *Adversaria*. These cover the years 1715-1765 and consist of numerous geometrical problems interspersed with exercises in algebra and astronomy, as well as occasional accounts of financial transactions.

Additional comments

Simson also made many discoveries of his own in geometry and the Simson line is named after him. However the Simson line does not appear in his work but Poncelet in *Propriétés Projectives* says that the theorem was attributed to Simson by Servois in the Gergonne's Journal. It appears that the theorem is due to William Wallace.

The University of St Andrews awarded Simson an honorary Doctorate of Medicine in 1746.

In 1753 Simson noted that, as the Fibonacci numbers increased in magnitude, the ratio between adjacent numbers approached the golden ratio, whose value is

$(1 + \sqrt{5})/2 = 1.6180 \ldots$

Article by: *R A Rankin*, Glasgow

Transcripts: A Topographical Dictionary of Scotland. Originally published by S. Lewis, London, 1846.

Kilbride, West

¶

KILBRIDE, WEST, a parish, in the district of Cunninghame, county of Ayr, 5½ miles (N. W. by W.) from Saltcoats; containing 1885 inhabitants. This place derives its name from the dedication of its church, which was anciently an appendage of the monastery of Kilwinning, to St. Bride, a virgin occupying a distinguished rank in the Scottish calendar. In 1263, it was the scene of a severe conflict with a party of Norwegians that had made a descent on the coast of Largs under Haco, who was here attacked and defeated by a body of Scottish forces commanded by Sir Robert Boyd, ancestor of the Kilmarnock family. As a reward for his conduct in this instance, Boyd obtained a grant of land in Cunninghame; and his services as the firm adherent of Bruce procured him the lands of Kilbride and Ardneil, in this parish. The parish is advantageously situated on a peninsular projection in the Frith of Clyde, below the Cumbray islands, of which the smaller, for all ecclesiastical purposes, is included within its limits; it is six miles in length and two and a half in average breadth, and comprises about 11,000 acres, of which 7500 are arable, and 3000 pasture and waste. The surface is diversified with hills forming part of the continued chain of the Renfrewshire range, and of which the highest within the parish, called Kame Hill, has an elevation of nearly 1000 feet above the level of the sea. There are also many hills of smaller elevation, partly cultivated, and some nearly to their summit; and others in detached situations, of which the chief are Law, Ardneil, and Tarbert. The coast is low, consisting of shelving rocks of sandstone, with the exception of the promontory of Portincross, which is precipitous, terminating in a point called Ardneil Bank, or Goldberrie Head. The sands of Southanan extend for two miles in the north of the parish; immediately to the south of them, the coast for nearly a mile is formed of the promontory, a wall of rock rising to the height of 300 feet, and separated from the sea only by a narrow slip of verdant land. This majestic rampart, of which the base is thickly studded with coppice wood, interwoven with oak, ash, hazel, and hawthorn, has a romantic grandeur of appearance as seen from the water: three detached cliffs that rise above the general height have obtained the appellation of the Three Sisters. To the south of the promontory is the bay of Ardneil, of semicircular form, the shores of which, a fine compact sand, afford a delightful promenade, with every facility for bathing, for which this part of the coast is peculiarly adapted. The Gourock, Kilbride, Southanan, and Fairly burns, which have their rise in the eastern confines, flow in various directions through the parish into the Frith. The Southanan, in part of its course between banks richly wooded, forms a pleasingly picturesque cascade; the others are not distinguished by any particular features. Numerous springs are also found in different parts, affording an abundant supply of excellent water.

¶

The soil in the lower lands near the coast is in some places a rich loam, in others sandy and gravelly; the higher parts are of very inferior quality, generally thin, cold, and spongy moor, with the exception of some portions around the bases of the hills, which are of loam mixed with calcareous earth. The crops are, wheat, oats, barley, a small quantity of rye, beans, peas, potatoes, turnips, and carrots; but, as well from the nature of the soil, as from the situation of the parish in a wide manufacturing district, most of the farms are appropriated to the dairy. The number of milch-cows, which are of the Ayrshire or Cunninghame breed, is about 600, and of cattle of other kinds, 800: the number of horses reared is exceedingly small; about 2500 sheep, chiefly of the black-faced breed, are pastured on the moorlands and hills, and 250 swine kept. The chief produce of the dairy is cheese, of which great quantities are sent to the neighbouring markets, where it is sold under the appellation of Dunlop cheese. The system of agriculture is advanced, and the implements of husbandry generally of the most approved kind. The farm buildings, which were formerly of a very inferior description, have in many instances been rebuilt in a substantial and commodious style, and on most of the farms threshing-mills have been erected; the lands are all inclosed with hedges and ditches in the lower parts of the parish, and in some of the higher parts with stone dykes. The woods are of small extent, not more than 150 acres, and of these about one-third is coppice wood; the remainder consists of oak, ash, plane, elm, and beech, with a little fir. On some of the lands are fine specimens of old timber; but they are comparatively few, and in general the proper management of plantations is little regarded, though a great quantity of land, which, from its quality, is incapable of cultivation, might, on account of its favourable situation, be advantageously appropriated to this use. The substrata are, sandstone of brown and red colour, whinstone porphyrytic and basaltic, some slight veins of limestone, and a white sandstone intermixed with quartz. The rateable annual value of the parish is £9805.

¶

Underbank, a pleasing villa, recently erected near the site of the old mansion-house of the barony of Southanan, is finely situated in a richly-wooded demesne. Crosby has been lately restored in harmony with its original character, and is now a tolerable residence. Hunterston is beautifully situated at some distance, towards the sea, from the ancient mansion-house, which is now occupied by a tenant, and of which the square tower is still in good preservation. The village is about a mile from the sea, in a small secluded vale watered by the Kilbride burn, which in its course gives motion to five different mills, two for grinding oats, one for bark, one for grinding charcoal, and one for dressing flax. There is a public library, supported by subscription; and a post-office has been established under good regulation. The tanning of leather was once carried on here, affording employment to a dozen persons; but the inhabitants are now chiefly occupied in weaving for the manufacturers of Glasgow and Paisley, in which more than one hundred handlooms are constantly at work; and a large portion of the female population are engaged in sewing and embroidering muslins. A few lobsters are taken in the season, and sent to the Glasgow market, and herrings are occasionally taken in large quantities; the other fish are, cod, whiting, mackerel, and a few others, but they are not in any great abundance. The streams that flow through the parish abound in trout of good quality. A small quay was constructed at Portincross some years since, at the expense of the proprietor; it is accessible at high water to vessels of forty or fifty tons. The Clyde steamers from Glasgow to Ardrossan and Ayr pass by the coast, and facility of intercourse with the neighbouring towns is maintained by good roads, of which the turnpike-roads to Greenock and Portpatrick run

through the whole length of the parish, and a line from the village communicates with the road to Glasgow at the village of Dalry.
¶
The parish is in the presbytery of Irvine and synod of Glasgow and Ayr; the minister's stipend is £202. 12., with a manse, and a glebe valued at £13. 12. per annum. The church, situated on a gentle eminence in the centre of the village, was rebuilt in 1732; subsequent additions have been made to it, and within the last few years an aisle has been erected by voluntary subscriptions. It is now adapted for a congregation of 800 persons. There are places of worship for members of the Free Church and the United Secession. The parochial school affords instruction to about 130 children; the master has a salary of £27. 17. 8., with £40 fees, and a house and garden. There are three friendly societies, which tend to diminish the number of applications for parochial relief. Along the steep banks opposite the sea are several circular mounds, at unequal distances, called the Castle Hills; the area on the summit, about forty feet in diameter, is inclosed with walls of undressed stone. Their origin is uncertain; by some they are ascribed to the Danes, by others referred to a more remote period. Tumuli have been explored in various places, containing urns with calcined bones and ashes; and in forming the new line of road along the coast, some few years since, four entire urns, rudely formed of coarse red clay, were dug out of a stratum of gravel. A silver brooch, of exquisitely delicate workmanship, and bearing an inscription in Runic characters, was found at Hunterston a few years since. The walls of the ancient castle of Portincross are still tolerably entire, and form a singularly romantic object, standing on a ledge of rock projecting into the sea; it is supposed to have been a residence of the Scottish kings. One of the large ships of the Spanish armada sank near the promontory, in ten fathoms of water; and an iron cannon which, with others, was recovered from the wreck, is still remaining on the beach: the arms of Spain, and a crown engraved on it, may be faintly traced. On an eminence overlooking the village of Kilbride, are the remains of a very stately tower called Law Castle, the walls of which are in perfect preservation. Dr. Robert Simson, professor of mathematics in the university of Glasgow, and the well known translator of Euclid, is thought to have been a native of the parish. General Robert Boyd, lieutenant governor of Gibraltar during the siege of that fortress in

1782, was born here; and it is supposed that John Hunter, the celebrated physician, was descended from the Hunterston family of this place.

Monuments: Tay Bridge Disaster Monument

The office of LAH Travel sits directly under the Tay Bridge disaster monument which was erected by the good people of West Kilbride in 1880 as a mark of respect to the 59 folks that lost their life.

At approximately 7:15 p.m. on the stormy night of 28 December 1879, the central navigation spans of the Tay bridge collapsed into the Firth of Tay at Dundee, taking with them a train, 6 carriages and

75 souls to their fate.

At the time, a gale estimated at Beaufort force 10/11 was blowing down the Tay estuary at right angles to the bridge. The collapse of the bridge, only opened 19 months and passed safe by the Board of Trade, sent shock waves through the Victorian engineering profession and general public.

The disaster is one of the most famous bridge failures and to date it is still one of the worst structural engineering failures in the British Isles.

The first Tay rail bridge was completed in February 1878 to the design of Thomas Bouch. Bouch was responsible for the design, construction and maintenance of the bridge. Most of his bridges were lattice girders supported on slender cast iron columns braced with wrought iron struts and ties, such as the Belah Viaduct in the photograph to the right. The building of the Tay bridge culminated in him being knighted.

The Tay bridge was nearly two miles long, consisting of 85 spans and at the time was the longest bridge in the world. The spans carried a single rail track; 72 of these were supported on spanning girders below the level of the track; the remaining 13 navigation spans were spanning girders above the level of the track (i.e. the train runs through a tunnel of girders).

These "high girders", as they were known, were 27 ft high with an 88 ft clearance above the high water mark. It was these spans which fell. Most of the girders below track level, all of which remained standing, were transferred to the present Tay rail bridge. At the time of the collapse Bouch was working on the design of the proposed Forth Bridge. In consequence, the design of the bridge was transferred to Benjamin Baker and Sir John Fowler.

In 1880, the town council of West Kilbride decided to erect a monument to the people who lost their lives and the ball was affixed to the top of the building as shown.

A History of West Kilbride in 100 Objects: the Seamill Post Box

Its early March, 1953. Rumours abound the political hotbed of nationalist intent of Seamill, that the next post box to be blown up, will be the one outside the wee village post office. Not by stealth do the Post Office swoop down and change the EIIR box to the sorry plastic one we see to this day. If a bomb were to be left in this box, no metal shrapnel would spread out across the busy A78 road or into the busy wee post office.

How had this all started? Elizabeth, the Queen had taken the name of Elizabeth II, and the first postbox in Scotland bearing her initials EIIR had been unveiled by Sir Winston Churchill in Inch, near Edinburgh.

On 28 November 1952, an official party assembled at the junction of Gilmerton Road and Walter Scott Avenue in Edinburgh's newly-built Inch housing estate to formally unveil Scotland's first 'E II R' pillar box. What at first appeared as a perfectly appropriate and harmless recognition of the new head of state quickly descended into a cause of national outrage leading to wide scale media coverage, debates in the House of Commons and intense police surveillance.
The problem was that the Tudor Queen Elizabeth I had never ruled over Scotland, therefore the suggestion that there could be a Queen Elizabeth II was considered grossly inaccurate and unacceptable to many Scots.

Shortly before the official unveiling of the pillar box, a pressure group had written to a number of officials to question the legality of using the E II R symbol. The authorities were, therefore, aware of the controversy, and five police officers were present at the unveiling ceremony.

Under attack

Despite the box receiving special police attention, within thirty-six hours the E II R symbol had been defaced with tar. A week later a parcel containing gelignite was found inside the post box, and on 2 January 1953, a postal worker found another explosive charge.

All was quiet for the next few weeks until, on 7 February, two workmen saw a man vandalising the box with a sledgehammer wrapped in a sack. The attacker ran off and the damaged pillar box door had to be removed for repair.
Blown apart

Finally, on 12 February 1953 at around 10pm, the Inch was rocked by an explosion that could be heard a mile away. The three-month-old post box had been completely blown apart courtesy of a gelignite bomb. The next day a small Lion Rampant was discovered draped across its smouldered ruins. A brand new pillar box appeared soon after with no sign of E II R.

The E II R issue was debated in the House of Commons and even in court, but attempts to challenge the Queen's right to be declared as Elizabeth II across the United Kingdom proved to be unsuccessful. A further statement by the Crown would declare that the Royal title

of the new monarch should reflect the highest number from either the Kingdom of England or the Kingdom of Scotland. However, the bombing incident had caused significant distress among Inch residents, who made it clear that any future erection carrying the E II R identification would not be welcome. To avoid any further troubles Scottish pillar boxes, mail vans and other post office paraphernalia would carry the Crown of Scotland from then on.

Seamill

A rumour developed in Seamill, that the group that had bombed the Inch post box, were now planning a similar dastardly scheme on the West Coast. The Police had heard indications that a post box somewhere in Inverclyde was being targeted, and possibly the Seamill one. The Seamill box sat on a busy road, in a wealthy area, in relative darkness at night and with a minimal police presence. There was every possibility that if another box was to be blown up, this could be the one.

The post office also took these rumours seriously, and quickly moved to take the existing post pox away. A new "safer" plastic postbox replaced it. The new postbox as shown above has no EIIR insignia and has only the Scottish crown on it.

The Post Office had long since closed, and of course the bombing never happened, but occasionally, just occasionally, you can see the post box tilting to one side as if listening to the rumours and waiting to be released from it's solitary existence.

Derivation of Place Names: Bowfield Road

"Bow" is old Scots, meaning "cattle" and so it seems reasonable that this name will mean "Cattle Field". This area of land was noted on Bleau's map of 1655 as "Ridsheelis" and Isaac Jackson postulates that this name may well have come from the old Norse "skjol" meaning shelter, due to the old agricultural worker cottages that once stood on the land.

In the late 17th Century, the name became shortened to Ridshiels, but through the early part of that century wealthy landowners threw the workers off of prime grazing land (the "West Kilbride Clearances"). As new farming techniques developed and the yield on crops got better, plus a demand for flax by the new weaving industry got greater, the agricultural cottages were reoccupied, grew in number and size. By this new development they became known as the "Bowfield Cottages" or "Cattlefield Cottages" as they are translated.

The main farming family of this land, the Caldwells (see Caldwell Road), grew in wealth during those 17th and 18th centuries and settled on one larger manor house entitled Bowfield House. Bowfield House sat near to the footpath now connecting Bowfield Road and Glenbryde Road.

Ultimately the cottages and Bowfield House were demolished at the end of the 19th Century to allow the development of new houses and the road, which was therefore named Bowfield Road.

Derivation of Place Names: Paton's Brae

This is the section of the hill of Main Street that Kirktonhall sits upon. According to Lamb it was named after a particular weaver who once had a cottage on the hill. This would have probably been where the doctor's surgery now stands. Next door to the right as we look at the surgery from the Main Street, was what he described as a "beggars howff".

History: A Short History of The Seamill Cooperative Home (1890-1912)

The first call upon the Scottish Co-operative Women's Guild occurred when it was only fourteen months old. The claims of the newly-launched scheme of the Co-operative Convalescent Seaside Homes at West Kilbride had become most pressing, and the promoters were in grave doubt as to the possibility of carrying out their noble ideas for want of the necessary funds;

During the autumn of 1890, the idea occurred to a few of the members of the committee of Ayrshire Co-operative Conference Association that the time had arrived when the Co-operative movement in Scotland ought to make an advance of such a nature as would lift it from the position of being, to a very large extent, a movement existing only for the purpose of making and dividing profits. They considered that an effort should, without delay, be made to induce societies to devote a portion of their rapidly-growing wealth to bestowing upon their members a new and higher class of benefits through the development of a humanitarian phase of Co-operation, and by this means raise the movement to a higher level than mere commercialism. In their opinion, the life and soul and glory of the Co-operative movement consisted in the ideal of ameliorating, if it could not totally remove, the suffering, the misery, and the sorrow of the poor struggling masses of the nation; to make the lives of the poorest of the people contented, sweet and happy;

and just in proportion as it endeavoured to reach this ideal would the brightness of it's fame and honour increase; but in proportion as it set this ideal aside, or delayed in trying to realise it, so would the brightness of its glory and prestige and its claims upon the community decline.

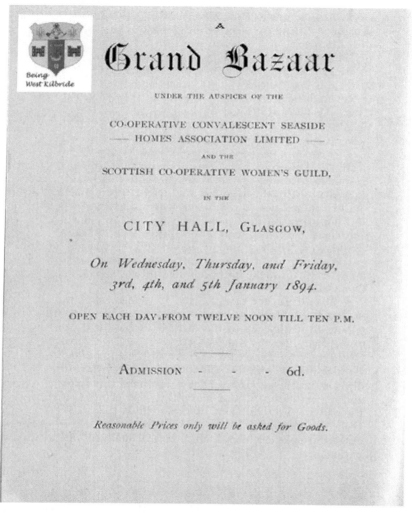

A

Grand Bazaar

UNDER THE AUSPICES OF THE

CO-OPERATIVE CONVALESCENT SEASIDE
—— HOMES ASSOCIATION LIMITED ——

AND THE

SCOTTISH CO-OPERATIVE WOMEN'S GUILD,

IN THE

CITY HALL, GLASGOW,

On Wednesday, Thursday, and Friday,
3rd, 4th, and 5th January 1894.

OPEN EACH DAY FROM TWELVE NOON TILL TEN P.M.

ADMISSION -   -   - 6d.

Reasonable Prices only will be asked for Goods.

At the quarterly meeting of the Ayrshire Conference Association, held at Ardrossan in January 1891, Mr George Seymour, Kilwinning, read an excellent paper, in which he set forth the claims for the erection of a Seaside Home by the Societies of the West of

Scotland. The appeal of the paper was most favourably received, and a committee was appointed to co-operate with any similar committee that would help in the raising of funds to build and furnish a Seaside Home. A site, situated on one of the most sheltered spots on the upper part of the Ayrshire Coast – viz., at Seamill, fully a mile from West Kilbride, and about three miles from Ardrossan – was secured; and on the 16th September 1893, Mr William Maxwell, Chairman of the Scottish Co-operative Wholesale Society, cut the first sod and was made the recipient of a souvenir of the occasion from Mrs McLean, president of the Guild. It soon became evident

FESTIVAL AND EXHIBITION OF WORK, 1904.

that if the Homes were to be erected and furnished in an manner worthy of the movement, a much larger sum of money would require to be raised, and the members of the Women's Guild suggested a Bazaar as a likely way to raise the money. This Bazaar, then, was really the first effort of the Guild, and with unsparing effort they carried it to a success that was undreamt of by the promoter of the scheme.

There were thirteen stalls at the Bazaar, ten of them being stocked with goods made up by the members of the branches, the others being the "Floral Stall", the "Productive Societies' Exhibition" and the "Committee's Stall".

This function was the means of consolidating the members of the Guild, and gave them their first recognition in a public way as a power in the Co-operative movement. Indeed, "one aim, one object" is the best description of how the work was got through, because the hours spent in knitting and sewing and fancywork of all descriptions could only have been sacrificed by people who wee thoroughly in earnest. Although societies gave contributions of material to the Guildswomen to make up for the Bazaar, there must have been considerable contributions from individuals (many of whom had not a great income to draw upon) to attain the handsome result. The hall being public property and in great demand, it could only be had on the days booked, and preparations had to be made expeditiously. Therefore, on the opening day, 3rd January 1894, a large and willing staff of men and women were on the ground by five o'clock in the morning, many of them having to travel a considerable distance. In some instances societies provided brakes to take the Guildswomen to the hall, but in the majority of cases they had to walk. Some there were who stayed overnight with friends so that they might be in time, and one pioneer actually actually rose at three o'clock.

The Homes were formally opened on Saturday 27th June 1896, and Mr Robert Duncanson, chairman of the Homes Association, performed the ceremony in presence of a large gathering of representative Co-operators, many enthusiastic Guildswomen being among them.

The memorial-window gifted by Duncan Bell (Brother of the President of the Scottish Co-operative Women's Guild, Mrs McLean) is on the main staircase facing the entrance, and shows Messrs George Seymour, W.B. Flockhart, James Deans, J. Inglis, R. Duncanson, (who originated the idea of the Homes) and William Barclay (the donor of £2,000 to the building fund). The window is a beautiful one and around the two top figures with clasped hands are leaves which denote "Peace", the two central figures having the "Scotch Thistle" surrounding them, suggestive of "Patriotism", while over the two bottom figures is the horn of "Plenty".

"Peace"
"Patriotism"
"Plenty"

Documents: The Public Roup Flier 1893

A roup was a public auction and an upset price is now known as a reserve i.e. the lowest price this building will sell for (£200 in this instance). I don't think the "Good Templars Hall" is the Masonic Lodge now on Arthur Street, since I believe Arthur Street was built to accommodate the new West Kilbride Institute building (Village Hall) in 1900. Arthur Street was named after Baron Glenarthur who paid for the Village Hall, and the title remains in place to this day.

Defining West Kilbride: West Kilbride Fair Day

Pont (1604) "Kill-Bryde 1 of Februarii"

Dogie (1874) Addendum: This fair, commonly called Brydes day, was originally held on the first day of the month. "In latter times the day has been changed to the second Tuesday. Fairs on Festival days invariably originated with the clergy, who derived certain emoluments from them, and they were usually celebrated within the church and its precincts. In this place, the travelling merchants or packman, even within the present century, continued to exhibit their wares within the churchyard" (Statistical Account Killbryde). There is another fair on the Friday preceding that of Largs.

Note. Kilbryde was a settlement under the abbey of Kilwinning. The fair day of Kilwinning was typically the first Monday of February.

A History of West Kilbride in 100 Objects: A 1950's BB Lifeboy Badge

In October 1926 the Boys' Brigade united with The Boys' Life Brigade. The merger also prompted the abandonment of dummy drill rifles that had been used in The Boys' Brigade, due to the Life Brigade's objection to use of weapons or their representations. The Junior organisation of the Boys' Brigade prior to 1926 was called 'The Boy Reserves' but after amalgamation the juniors were called 'The Life Boys'. The name came from the fact that the junior reserve of The Boys' Life Brigade had been known as 'Lifeboys' (all one word). The Life Boys remained as the 'Junior Reserve of the Boys' Brigade until 1966 when the name was changed to 'The Junior Section'.

1st West Kilbride Boys Brigade Company has always had a vibrant Lifeboys then Junior Section. A younger age group of the company is now known as "the Anchor Boys".

This enamel badge would have been worn on the cap of a Life Boy during the 1950's in West Kilbride.

Derivation of Place Names: Avondale

In my book "A History of the West Kilbride Town Coat of Arms", I describe how Avondale Road and Avondale Lodge got their name. They came from the birth place of local business man, John Dunlop. I print the details below.

John Dunlop was a licensed grocer in West Kilbride from about 1885 until 1907 and was the designer of the second and third major variations of the town coat of arms in 1903 and 1907 respectively.
In 1861, John Dunlop was born to father John and mother Agness (sic) who were farmers at Whiteshawgate, Avondale in Lanarkshire. In the family there were seven children – John having an elder sister Helen, two elder brothers Robert and Sam and three younger sisters – Maggie, Mary and Marion. Being the third son, farming opportunities were somewhat limited and John left school at the age of 15 to become a grocery assistant.

During the second half of the 1870's and early 1880's, John worked as an assistant under a Miss Agness Graham of Moffat. It seems he worked well and in about 1885 an opportunity arose to set up his own licensed grocery business at 65 Main Street, West Kilbride. Where James Dalzell Simpson operated a tourist focused business selling books, newspapers and giftware, John Dunlop aimed to sell the essentials through his licensed grocery and then added on tourist items as an adjunct – such as postcards and small high margin giftware items. At about the same time Alexander Smith Todd, one of the Todd Brothers (see below) arrived in West Kilbride from a small village in Lanarkshire not twelve miles from where John Dunlop originated. These two retailers were almost exactly the same age and immediately struck up a great friendship.

In the late 1880's his sister Helen came over to help in the grocery business and they both stayed on the Main Street. By the early 1990's John had met Eliza Wilson from Dreghorn and they were married. Eliza had been born in 1877 the only daughter to a wealthy farmer John Wilson and his wife Jessie.

When Eliza was about 6 and Jessie was only 39, John died suddenly leaving his entire estate to Jessie. The grandfather was still alive and tried his best to help out, but the substantial farm along with the rest of the family estate was too much for the two ladies and the old man to manage and they decided to sell up. It was then that Eliza met John Dunlop and they decided to get married.

During the first years of their marriage, Eliza and John lived in the Main Street premises, with Eliza's mother Jessie. However, coming from a wealthy farming background, Jessie soon struck up a friendship with Lady Jane Hunter of Hunterston and several other well to do locals, such as those who might be resident in Highthorn House at the time. It would therefore be important that they invest in a home more in keeping with their new social status, and therefore they decided to build a substantial new house.

The house the Dunlops built was "Avondale Lodge" which was on the road to the Hunterston estate, by way of Highthorn. They had listed this as their address in the 1901 census. It is still there to this day. In 1897, when the cemetery was extended and the approach road widened to enable two horse drawn carriages to go side by side up the hill, the road was named "Avondale Road".

Avondale was of course the birthplace of John Dunlop in Lanarkshire.

Derivation of Place Names: Caldwell

The derivation of Caldwell may be in two parts. Firstly, "cald" is a change from keld (as in the name of the town Dunked)* and the original kjeld has the Scandinavian meaning "kettle" or "caldron". The second part of the name is simple English and refers to a well or spring. There is a hill nearby called Caldron-Gattle but I suspect that this is simply coincidental as Caldwell is a prolific name throughout Ireland and following the settlers into Scotland.

The Caldwell family were farmers of some long standing in the village. They were probably distant cousins of the Mure family of the Caldwell estate in Renfrewshire. Certainly there are marital records of a direct relationship in the 15th Century between the Mure family and the Semple family of the Southannan estate.

They were also connected by marriage to the Boyd family, and again in the 15th century we see mention of the Montgomeries. The complicated relationships from the 15th century to the 19th do need teasing out at some point – but we do know that the Barony Parish Church had its memorial stone laid on August 10th 1872 by Colonel William Mure of Caldwell+. The large Caldwell estate was near Uplawmoor in Renfrewshire and Lugton in Ayrshire.

The Caldwell landholding in the 19th Century encompassed the area from the glen, through Bowfield Road and right down to Caldwell Road, possibly ending at Pantonville Road (Borough Faulds). The farm was entitled Bowfield (prior to which it was called Ridshiels) and the family home was Bowfield House which was situated at end of what is now Bowfield Road. It was demolished in the early part of the 20th Century to make way for the new housing developments on Caldwell and Bowfield Road.

Plot 84 of the Barony Church Graveyard has a grave marker stone which states:

CALDWELL

In memory of WILLIAM CALDWELL late
Farmer in Bowfield who d. 13th November
1835 a. 79 years
Also his sons WILLIAM who d. 22nd SEPTR
1841 a. 27 years
And ANDREW who d. 25th June 1847 a. 34 years
And his wife MARGARET BOYD who d. 1st Septr 1849
Aged 79 Years; also of his GrandDaughter
MARGARET BOYD STEEL who d. 20th Feby 1855
8 years; and his son
JOHN CALDWELL who d. 17th Decr. 1859
61 years

History: Naming the Portencross Armada Wreck

After a four hundred and thirty year wait, a new chapter is dawning on the history of the Spanish Armada. Today we announce the name of the ship wrecked on 8th August 1588 off Portencross as *El Espíritu Santo* – a small two masted ship known as a patache, from the Squadron of Andalusia of the mighty Spanish Armada. For all this time El Espírito Santo has been listed as missing at sea. Thanks to a new book by local historian, Stephen Brown, we are now able to declare the lost ship found.

In "The Portencross Armada Conspiracy (and how the Spanish landed in Ayrshire)" (The Transparent Publishing Company, 2015), the author explains that a patache was generally expected to carry about 40 soldiers and sailors, and ten cannon. The Portencross one was vastly overladen with 112 men and 43 cannon – probably one of the major reasons why she eventually foundered and sank only one mile from the coast.

The Armada cannon recovered in 1740, as it remains in October 2015, in a private garden

In the south of England, on *exactly the same day*, the full Armada was facing the English fleet. By the 9th of August they were dispersed and had started sailing north on their epic journey home. *El Espírito Santo* was not one of these many ships of the dispersed Armada, fighting for survival. Stephen Brown, using uncovered Spanish and Scottish State records from 1588, shows how an advance party of Spanish Diplomats from the Armada, and plotting Scottish nobles, were sent to speak to King James VI in the hope of convincing him to launch an army against the English. If he refused, the great Catholic Lords of the West of Scotland were expected to rise up, overthrow the King, and secure our nation for the counter-Reformation.

As news of the Spanish defeat was beginning to arrive in Edinburgh, James had all the conspirators quickly arrested. The Spanish were tortured to reveal details of their plot, then executed. The Scottish participators were detained on a charge of treason. One Lochwinnoch Colonel escaped to Spain. Others having been found guilty of treason, were then forgiven by the King. Most were dead within a few years of the affair, taking the secret of the Portencross Armada Conspiracy to their grave.

In his book, Stephen Brown also gives many new details of the 1740 salvage operation to find the cannon of the *El Espírito Santo*. The bronze cannon found were melted down, but many of the Armada iron cannons remain dotted about the west coast, and can still be seen to this day sitting outside.

The book also explains that the sunken ship's hold should still contain twenty three Armada falconet cannon.

As in almost every Spanish Armada wreck, there are also rumours of great treasure to be found. Certainly there are details contained within the book of a considerable amount of missing treasure, but was it taken before the ship sank? Or did Sir Francis Drake himself take it?

The story of *El Espíritu Santo* is not one of a simple shipwreck. It is a tale of conspiracy and intrigue, and of unscrupulous characters from both the Elizabethan and Georgian ages. Nor is the story over. Archaeologists are currently discussing whether to try excavate the site, and now with the identification of *El Espíritu Santo*, a great deal of further information is likely to emerge.

A fragmentary and decayed letter in the Scottish State Papers from Sir Henry Woddryngton dated 11th August, 1588, states:

"ay last in the mor ... the Spanish fleet to the Fryth ... there cast anchor and launched out ... cockboat with 12 or 14 men in her, all Spaniards, directed to Colonel Simple, who ... conveyed to him safely to Edinburgh. After conference with him, the town understanding that they were Spaniards committed them to ward; who confessed that in that ship there is about 100 soldiers with victual and munition."

Competition Time: The Seven Ancient Wonders of West Kilbride

So I started a wee album called "A History of West Kilbride in 100 Objects" which I'm messing about with - maybe it will become a new book or just sit here. But now it's your chance to have a think. I want to know what are the:

SEVEN ANCIENT WONDERS OF WEST KILBRIDE ?

To be nominated, an item must be fixed (i.e. not a van or a person), over 250 Years Old (older the better) and not a private dwelling (so as not to cause any undue upset when the tour bus stops outside and a billion chinese make entry). Nominate your suggestions here (I already have eight in mind but I want your ideas) before Christmas.

Then, by Boxing day all being well, if folks are interested, I shall upload a photo and possibly a short history of the item (if I know anything about it) into an album headed "The Seven Ancient Wonders of West Kilbride" and you will be invited to vote by hitting "like" against each image you select - vote for as many or as few as you like but you can only vote once for each item obviously.

The top seven ancient items at the stroke of midnight on Hogmanay (and we may have a Facebook Party!) will appear in the members choice album as the "Official" Seven Ancient Wonders of West Kilbride.

Nominations at the middle of November:

1. Portencross Castle c. (1375)
2. Cup and Ring markings (Stone Age)
3. Kirktonhall (c.1660)
4. Law Castle (c. 1474)
5. The Cat Linn (c. 1623)
6. The Old Coach Road (medieval)
7. The Kirktonhall Sundial (c. 1660)
8. The Hunterston Brooch (c. 10th Century)
9. Crosbie Tower (medieval in parts)
10. The Sea Mill (17th Century?)
11. Auld Hill Vitrified Fort (Bronze Age, c 1500-2000AD)
12. Glenfoot Double Fort (Bronze Age, c 1500-2000AD)
13. The Portencross Armada Cannon (c. 1580)

Excluded: Private residences (e.g. The Fort); Under 250 Years Old (The Simson Monument, The Gasworks); Natural Occurrences (Whispering sands of Ardneil, Law Hill, The Glen);

Derivation of Place Names: Alton

Alton refers to the position of the area within the village.

"Alton" is a reference to days gone by where it would have led to the "Auld Town". In many of the names of West Kilbride, like most other lowland towns of Scotland "…ton" will refer to town, taken from the middle English for example Hunterston, Boydston, Kirkton. At times "ton" can refer to a "hill" as in Yerton which would be middle english for "Yer" – Over and "ton" – the hill. In this instance Alton will refer to the "Auld Town" because Alton Street points directly towards Ritchie Street and runs away Headrigg Road.

"Headrigg" is a medieval name meaning simply the head of the "riggs" and so it may be assumed that this is very much an old part of the town.

The centre of West Kilbride remains organised very much on medieval riggs basis. A ring was the width of one dead man lying down – basically about six feet. When walking up the Main Street of West Kilbride (the Auld Town) one notes that many of the properties are multiples wide of that six feet measurement. This is because parcels of land for sale were originally based on riggs.

Derivation of Place Names: Arthur Street

Arthur Street was laid specifically to accommodate the new West Kilbride Institute which was completed in 1900. It was named in honour of James Arthur of Carlung who gifted the Paisley Co-operative Home (now Community Centre) to the village. James Arthur was the Chairman of the company he founded – James Arthur & Co. Limited – a clothing wholesalers based in Queen Street in Glasgow.

His son, Matthew Arthur, went on to become a director of several railway companies and was Chairman of the Western Infirmary for a while. He was also a Provincial Grand Master of the Ayrshire Freemasons – which is of course why the West Kilbride Lodge is situated on Arthur Street.

In 1903 Matthew Arthur was made the first Baron Glenarthur of Carlung and Bagshaw – taking the name of Glen from his mother's maiden name and Arthur from his patronymic. Matthew Arthur died in 1918.

The current Baron Glenarthur is the 4th – Simon Mark Arthur. He was born in 1944 and served in the Thatcher administration. He remains one of the last ninety elected hereditary peers in the House of Lords.

His son and heir Edward Alexander was born in 1973.

A History of West Kilbride in 100 Objects: The 1928 Jay Lascelles Town Crest

Between 1886 and 1928, a huge variety of town crests had developed from the original one of souvenir manufacturer, W.H.Goss. The West Kilbride Town Council therefore decided to engage the head of the Ardrossan

Academy Art Department, Jay Lascelles, to consider all the different types and come up with one final design for the West Kilbride Town

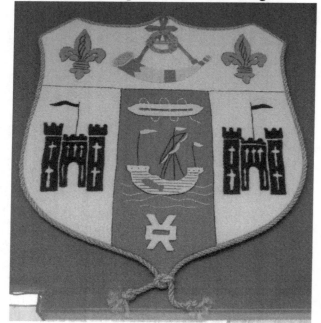

Crest. The final design accepted was the original W.H. Goss design and it was painted on a definitive shield as shown on the photograph attached.

For many years, this shield hung at the top of the curtain on the stage in the Main Hall of the Village Hall, but when the Museum was commissioned in the 1990's it was moved upstairs.

For many years, after the 1960's, it was the local history orthodoxy received from Peter A. MacNab that the Crest had in fact been originally designed by Lascelles and this false story was accepted until 2012 when Stephen Brown proved this to be false from postcard and crested china records.

The "orthodox" version of the Coat of Arms remains on show in the West Kilbride Museum above the doorway.

Derivation of Place Names: Portincross

Note that the name of Portencross (with an e) has a more modern derivation and is dealt with below.

When we are to consider where the name of *"Portincross"* came from, we must lay aside fanciful notions of Templar Knights, Roman Roads and Dead Kings of Scotland, and names such as "Portus Crucis", "The Port of the Cross", "Portus Cruies" and "Portcroash". The story of dead Kings of Scotland being transferred down a road to be buried in Iona was a 1799 "conjecture" (his words) of the Rev Oughterson, the Minister of Kilbride Parish in the "Old Statistical Account" 1. From that fateful conjecture, we have received all manner of legends, myths, tales and ideas for which there is absolutely no evidence. Even today, books are being sold in West Kilbride containing all manner of nonsensical tales. The derivation of Portincross is simply feudal – meaning the "port in Crosbie". Medieval Portincross

An early 20th Century, German printed, Stengel postcard showing a "General View of Portincross"

Sir Reginald de Craufurd was made the 1st hereditary Sheriff of Ayrshire in 1203 and married Margaret Loudoun (daughter and heir of James de Loudon). His son was Hugh Craufurd of Loudoun, and became the 2nd Sheriff of Ayrshire. According to Burkes Peerage it was this Craufurd that was granted the estate of Crosbie (medieval spelling was sometimes Corsbie or Corsby, but never Crosby as that was a famous singer in the 20th Century first name Bing) in Kilbride in 1226. It should be noted here that this was not per the local myth expounded in documents over the years that it was his son who was awarded Crosbie after the battle of Largs in 1263.

Hugh Craufurd of Loudoun had a son, confusingly also called Hugh Craufurd of Loudoun, but the latter was the 3rd Sheriff of Ayrshire. This Hugh Crawfurd was the famed hero of the battle of Largs against the Vikings in 1263. This Hugh Crawfurd, had a son, Reginald Craufurd of Loudoun and Crosbie, and in time Reginald became the 4th Sheriff of Ayrshire.

Reginald Craufurd was brother to William Wallace's mother, and is portrayed in the 15th Century poem by Blind Harry as being a father figure to William Wallace. The estate of Crosbie (Corsbie) is mentioned in the poem and Crosbie Castle or House is the subject of many a tale in West Kilbride folklore. Reginald was supposedly killed in the "Barns of Ayr" incident of 1297 which started William Wallace in his fight against subjugation, by the English. Here we do remember that this is all according to the one 15th Century poem and may or may not be factual.

Reginald Craufurd had three children, and this is where the Loudoun and cadet Crosbie branch of the Craufurd family separate. The first child, a son, was naturally named Reginald Crawfurd of Loudoun (the 5th Sheriff of Ayrshire) – this branch of the family, were later to become the Earls of Loudoun. A second son to Reginald was named William Craufurd and apparently became William Wallace's second in command only to be killed in battle in 1298.

The third son of Reginald Craufurd became the cadet branch of the family. This son was known as Hugh Craufurd of Crosbie and died in 1319, having given birth to yet another Reginald Craufurd in 1283.

This Reginald Crawfurd of Crosbie fought at the battle of Bannockburn with Robert the Bruce in 1314. In 1320 he was made the 1st Baron (Laird) of Auchenames in recognition of his services, and died in 1358 at the ripe old age of 75.

So here in 1320, the Craufurds own a substantial estate stretching from Crosbie in the east, to the lands of Auchenames on the coast. In terms we recognise today, they would have owned a large part of the Portencross peninsula bordering on Hunterston (Hunters town), West Kilbride, Seamill and, of course, the Crosbie estate. The senior title of Reginald Craufurd was the older Crosbie, which would later be split into a major and minor (cadet) branch of the family (see below). PORTINCROSS therefore was very simply – the port in Crosbie.

The old Portencross Post Office sign, now on display at the West Kilbride Museum in the Village Hall

Note: On the page where I discuss the slightly different derivation of PORTENCROSS (with an e), this is where it the two derivations cross. Portencross is derived from the local word "Pencross", referring to the piece of land to the north of the "Throughlet" which was the animal enclosure of the Crosbie estate – Pen of Crosbie (middle English "Penne" or Irish Gaelic "Peann" meaning animal enclosure). The two names Portincross and Pencross were conjoined by the Post Office around 1904 to form "Portencross".

The Throughlet – showing north to the area of Portencross called "Pencross". The cottage in the distance is Northbank.

Similarly, nowadays the street names of Corsehill, Corse Terrace, and the now defunct Cross Hill (the western end of Portencross Road on the hill) all derive their names from the Crosbie estate. Between 1320 and the turbulent times of the late 16th Century, when next documented land transfers take place, the place name of "port in Crosbie" became shortened through common use to "Portincross".
Portincross in the 16th Century

The lands of the Crosbie estate including Auchenames, remained together throughout the 14th and 15th centuries. In 1541, Thomas Craufurd, the seventh Lord of Auchenames died. He had three sons and a daughter – John Craufurd who became the 8th Laird of Auchenames, the cadet William Craufurd of Crosbie (thus splitting the estate in two), and Patrick Craufurd and Margaret Craufurd.

John Craufurd then died for Mary, Queen of Scots, in the battle of Pinkie Cleugh in 1547, returning the Barony of Auchenames to William who became the 9th Laird. William had a son called James Craufurd of Crosbie, who sadly died before his father – both dying in 1582. James had a daughter called Jean, who was then known as "the heiress of Crosbie".
On the early death of James, the Barony of Auchenames returned to Patrick Craufurd (the third son of Thomas above). Despite being

related, Patrick then married Jean "the heiress of Crosbie" to once again reunite the lands of Auchenames and Crosbie.

It was Jean who was responsible for the building of the bridge on Main Street at Bridgend, where we see she had her name carved with the date 1623.

Note: Margaret Craufurd married the Laird of Hunterston.
In a contract dated 1572 between two of the Boyd's of Ardneill (medieval Arnele, modern Ardneil) noted the land as:

"the ten merk land of Portincroce and Ardneill with the toure fortalice maneir place and thair pendiclis and pertinentis land"

In this document, Portincross had been spelled phonetically "Portincroce" as per many of the lowland Scots documents of these times. The similarity of the word "croce" to the latin word "cruce" meaning cross has lead to many flights of fancy over the subsequent years. We have read great stories of Templar Knights, Monks, and how the writer surely must have meant "crucis" – none of these conjectures have any evidence reported, as yet.

The Reverend Timothy Pont mapped much of Scotland in the late 1500's until about 1604. This map was used latterly by Blaeu to print. In the map, the castle and north are labelled "Poynt of Paincors". "Cors" referring to Corsbie – the alternative to the Crosbie estate. By the middle of the 17th Century, Blaeu had changed this to the more continental European, from whence he came, "Porten Kross".

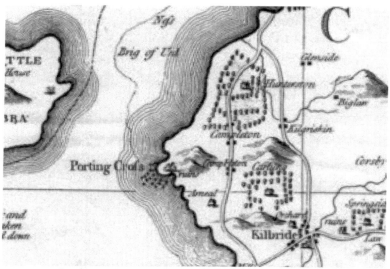

Andrew Armstrongs New Map of Ayrshire

In 1775, the name Portincross reappears in Andrew Armstrong's New Map of Ayrshire, now as "Porting Cross". This is interesting as it separates the word Cross – referring perhaps more clearly again to Corsbie, but may have been another confirmation that Rev Oughterson needed to make his flight of fancy. Even so, the area shown on the map is the Southern end of the peninsula where the castle sits. as we might expect from the details above – "Port of Crosbie".

In the early 19th Century, Thomson's Northern Part of Ayrshire Map and Aitken's Map of the Parish of West Kilbride refer to the whole area as "Portin Cross".

From the middle of the 19th Century, when the railway arrived, West Kilbride developed a huge number of streets and buildings to accommodate the burgeoning tourist industry. Corsehill and Corse Terrace on the original feudal lands of Corsbie were built and by the 1920's use of the name Crosshill had ceased (the hill from the corner of Corse Terrace and Portencross Road down to the A78 was actually called "Crosshill" until the early 20th Century (see postcard) but the name was changed to be an extension of Portencross Road, probably due to confusion with Corsehill). Corsehill, Corse Terrace and Crosshill would all have been part of the medieval Crosbie estate.

"The Coaches at Portincross" – An early Edwardian postcard showing the large horse drawn coaches bringing numbers people to the area.

The Post Office at "Portencross" – A postcard printed after the Post Office was opened.

The Portencross Post Office Hand Stamp from August 1904

In 1904, the village of Portincross was busy enough to merit a very small Post Office and have it's own hand stamp. The houses to the north of Portincross lay on the piece of land known locally as "Pencross" (see separate page detailing the derivation of this name). One such house – Northbank – Cottage was later to become infamous as the site of the "Portencross Murder".

Perhaps in the spirit of compromise, or perhaps by some accord of the residents of Portincross and Pencross, the Post Office hand stamp was produced using the name "Portencross". Thence forward picture postcards began to change from Portincross to Portencross.

By the time of publication of the J.G. Batholemew "Survey Map of Scotland" in 1912, the name "Portencross" was being used for the whole peninsula, excluding the Hunterston estate.

The Myths

From Rev Oughterson's "conjectures" (see above) came the idea of the dead kings of Scotland being brought down the well made route "from Edinburgh" to find their ultimate rest in Iona. The well made route was of course the drovers route worn over the centuries across the Crosbie Estate.

The word "cross" in Portincross does not, I say, refer to Templar Knights, despite a frantic attempt by modern masonry in Kilwinning to find some link to the order. There were a few Templar's on the west coast of Scotland, but these were through the inherited titles of the nobility. Robert the Bruce himself was such a hereditary Templar. Temple lands, such as in Dalry, were primarily connected with the nobility that inherited such honours. Scottish masonry is of course a modern invention largely made popular by the much later Earl of Eglington.

In 1966, the archaeologist Frank Newall, gave rise to a notion that there was a Roman Road to the north of Law Hill and driving through Thirdpart and Portencross to end at a supposed Roman Harbour and Pier. He named this road the "Avondale Road" (not to be confused with Avondale Road in West Kilbride – the history of which I discuss in my book "A History of the West Kilbride Town Coat of Arms"). The road was yet another fanciful notion. Old postcards show the road as "the Old Dalry Road" and it is plainly a drovers route to the north end of the Portencross peninsula. No archaeological evidence has yet been discovered to verify the road as Roman but it was agreed by professionals that its authentication did rather depend on the existence of the Roman harbour or pier.

Hunterston House, home of Lt Gen Sir Aylmer Hunter-Weston

The "Roman Pier" as shown on the Hunterston Estate website has been shown in 2015 to be a folly from the 18th Century by Wessex Archaeology who were conducting an investigation into the Hunterston Sands. The Harbour at Brigurds Point is an even later construction, probably built by Robert Hunter or the rather eccentric Lt Gen Sir Aylmer Hunter-Weston in the late 19th Century, and as suggested once again by our old pal Rev Oughterson in 1799. Hunter-Weston was known to have used the labour of the Royal Engineers to work on his estate prior to the first World War, and was also well known to take on fanciful notions of local history without much evidence (such as the false attribution of the name West Kilbride to a church of St Brigid located on the site of "The Fort" in Seamill).

Brigurds Point has for a long time been suggested as one of the possible mythical landing places of St Brigid in the area, but I believe the name was a localisation of "Brigands Point" as it was very much the location of a great deal of smuggling activity during the 16th and 17th century. It does not appear on any maps thus until the 20th Century, pointing the finger squarely at Hunter Weston.

1 "Hitherto, no satisfying account has been given of the origin of the name of this place. In the common language of the country, it is called Pencross, which is just a corruption of its proper ancient name, we may have only conjecture." Rev Mr Arthur Oughterson – The Statistical Accounts of Scotland, West Kilbride, Ayrshire, Account of 1791-99, Volume 12

Derivation of Place Names: Portencross (with an "e")

When we are to consider where the name of Portencross came from, we must lay aside fanciful notions of Templar Knights, Roman Road and Dead Kings of Scotland, and names such as "Portus Crucis", "The Port of the Cross", "Portus Cruies" and "Portcroash". These are all conjectural stories with absolutely no evidence in support. The answer, regrettably, is far more mundane and lies in the hands of the Post Office. The names of the village of "Portincross" and the more northerly land called "Pencross" were merged for the purposes of the new Post Office, established in Portincross Village around 1904. In a spirit of compromise, the residents of Northbank Cottage in Pencross, and the Villagers of Portincross, agreed that the Post Office Handstamp should say "Portencross".

Derivation of Place Names: Portincross (with an "i")

The name is as simple as "the port of Crosby" (or Corsbie if medieval). However, until the 20th Century, "Portencross" was actually spelled "Portincross", and referred to the land around the harbour of the castle. The area of land, farther to the north of the village and castle of Portincross, beyond what we know as "The Througlet", was an area known locally as "Pencross" at least until the earliest years of the 20th Century. "Pencross" derives (I believe) from "Pen" (middle English "Penne" or Irish Gaelic "Peann") meaning animal enclosure, and "Cross" being Crosbie i.e. the animal enclosure of the Crosby estate.

It is my humble opinion that animals would have been herded down the main drovers routes to the middle of the peninsula where the hills and sea afforded protection and security, and where the grazing was good. These routes have mistakenly been regarded as possible Roman Roads in recent years.

History: The Portencross Cannon

The Portencross cannon is a wrought iron medio sacre that came from the Spanish Armada patache "El Espiritu Santo" which sank one mile from Portencross harbour on the morning of the 8th August, 1588.

The full story of the ship, and the later salvage operation is detailed in my book entitled "The Portencross Armada Conspiracy".

This cannon was salvaged from the sunken ship by the famous diver Captain Jacob Roe in 1740.

Roe salvaged ten bronze cannon that were "disappeared" to Dublin to be melted down. Ten iron cannon were salvaged and dispersed to friends and supporters throughout the west. One remains at the McLean Museum in Greenock, another at the Duke of Argylls Inverary Castle and two at Lochryan House in Wigtonshire.

The wrought iron cannon shown above is what remains of the one given to the good people of Portencross for directing Roe to the wreck. It was manufactured around 1585 by London cannon manufacturers John and Richard Phillips of Cannonmakers Row.

The cannon, when originally given to Portencross was situated where the cottage is now to the right of the lane through to the castle. It had traditionally been pointing to the site of the wreck. In 1788, the cottage was built, and the cannon was moved to a site shown on this postcard, to the left of the castle, now pointing to the site of the wreck of another ship – the "Lady Margaret" which had sank in 1770.

Interestingly, the stone that the cannon sat on has since disappeared. It had the markings etched on it to inform where both wrecks were located out to sea.

In the 1990's, Hunterston Nuclear Power Station removed the cannon to sit at the front door of their headquarters. Then it was sent to Edinburgh to be desalinated – a process that did not yield any significant improvements. The cannon, in much worse condition as shown above, was then delivered back to Portencross wrapped in bandages. On removal of the bandages, years of layers started peeling off. Discussions still continue to this day on how to recover and display the cannon to the fullest.

A History of West Kilbride in 100 Objects: Cinerary Urns at Seamill

In 1830, then again in 1878, a number of funerary urns were discovered at the gate of "The Fort" in Seamill (a building that sits on a prehistoric site once known as "Castle Hill"). This is contrary to popular myth that they were found at the gate of the Seamill Hydro.

With the original find in 1830, Robert Hunter proposed to the Royal Society of Antiquaries of Scotland that these were early Christian cremations, and rumours developed of other skeletons having been found facing east to west to confirm this.

In 1878, as the new A78 road was being widened, again a number of cinerary urns were found. By this time, the Seamill Hydro was developing. The myth therefore began that these urns were probably from the original convent of St Brigid from whence the town got it's name.

A fabulous story developed regarding the landing of St Brigid and how the sea water around, and pumped into the baths within the Seamill Hydro.

As St Brigid was famous for healing, and for her convent on a hillock, the story gained some credibility in the local area.

Then in 1927, a further urn was discovered on the Hunterston Estate by a young agricultural worker and John Young, the sanitary engineer. Lieutenant-General Sir Aylmer Gould Hunter-Weston KCB DSO GStJ (23 September 1864 – 18 March 1940) was alerted to this find, and being well known for his eccentricities, he aligned these fines to the Seamill Fort ones with Brigurd Point being suggested as a possibility for the earliest landing of that saint – since it sounds a little like Brigid!

Following the revelation, by Frank Newall, that there may have been a Roman Road, Pier and Harbour near West Kilbride (myth!), the story of the urns quickly transferred to being mythically Roman. Pottery shards found in the Main Street and in Gateside Street have been variously attributed to the Romans in recent years.

In actual fact, the urns are much older. Alison Sheridan of the National Museums of Scotland has been able to date a number of similar urns to the Bronze Age and, by accurate carbon dating, to between 1500-2000 BC.

The various styles of cinerary urns found in Seamill and Hunterston

are all Bronze Age. They are usually found as we would regard, upside down with the base to the top. Consequently the base is usually missing but the bones inside are intact. Occasionally, there is evidence of small bronze items being buried with the person – such as jewellery or implements.

There is no shortage of Bronze Age sites throughout Scotland. Quite often these urns can be found standing upright in more solid structures that look like tombs – such as the "neolithic" tomb in Largs at the rear of Douglas Park –

sometimes also called "Haco's Tomb" (see below) and thereby also falsely attributing it to the viking ages.

History: The New Railway Station

On Wednesday, the 4th of April 1906, the first half of the new railway building opened. Much to the annoyance of the local businesses, and dignitaries, there was no opening ceremony whatsoever.

The old station building, which had been built in 1878, but was replaced in 1906.

An initial railway line had opened in to Ardrossan as a result of the endeavours of the 12th Earl of Eglinton, in 1831, but this was primarily for commercial mineral transportation, and was on a different gauge to passenger transports. The Ardrossan railway was taken over by the Glasgow and South Western Railway (G&SWR had formed in 1850) on the 24th July, 1854. The extension to West Kilbride was completed in 1878, but thereafter there was resistance to progress beyond.

A Fairlie Pier station was opened: the station roof was built using materials recovered from the temporary Dunlop Street station. Bitter and destructive competition for the ferry traffic to island locations developed, but the final stage to Largs was completed in 1885.

In 1878, there had been an opening ceremony. At that time, G&SWR were very aware of the coming battles to get the extension of the line through to Largs, and they had decided to make a grand show of the importance of this development. Since 1878, there had been a massive difference in the commercial life of the village, with over 10,000 people staying locally each weekend. Many new buildings had been established including three large church buildings on Main Street, all completed within 10 years of each other. The new village Institute (Village Hall) had opened in 1901 and the Co-operative homes, were in full business.

The new West Kilbride Station first opened in 1906 (note the gas lamp bottom right)

In fact, with hindsight, if we had to choose the busiest year for tourism in West Kilbride, we would probably select 1906. This was definitely the year when most postcards were sent from the village. 1906 was also the year the the Seamill Hydropathic became a private Limited company.

It was no wonder therefore, that in early 1906, the local businesses and other important people had expected a full replay of the grand opening ceremony of 1878. Instead, the new station was simply opened mid week to no fanfare whatsoever.

Derivation of Place Names: Faulds (Faulds Burn, Faulds Wynd, Burough Faulds)

This is lowland Scots meaning "fields". Burough Faulds relates to the area of land from Caldwell Road to the coast and was the former name of Pantonville Road.

Derivation of Place Names: Kilruskin

Kilruskin (Kilruskin Drive, South and North Kilruskin Farms) – Kilruskin is an estate of land near to Southannan. To get there, one would travel on the back road out of West Kilbride following Gateside Street, past the road to Crosbie, and towards Hunterston and Fairlie. The spelling of Kilruskin is a relatively new variation, up until the 1940's it was more popularly known as Kilrusken.

As in Kilbride, the "Kil" refers to a church, chapel or monastic cell. Kilruskin is very close to other landmarks of old celtic saints such as Cubrieshaw (St. Cuthbert's wood), Southannan (St. Inan) and indeed Portencross where several saints are supposed to have rested in austere circumstances in the caves under the three sister cliffs. It would therefore be natural to look for a St. Ruskin or Ronskan or similar. Often in our local history, we are apt to take on fanciful notions that St Brigid or St Ruskin visited us and established a celtic cell, convent or church.

In actual fact, what happened was as simple as this. An agricultural settlement would develop where groups of families would work the land together. When that settlement became of a significant size, a church (it was the Holy Roman Emperor Charlemagne that invented the Parish system) would be founded and it would be dedicated to a reasonably well known saint e.g. Kilbride - St Brigid, or some noble family e.g. Ardnele (Ardneil) was the toun of the Hunters which became Hunterstoun, or some ill met desire e.g. the abandoned 16th Century settlement behind Law Hill known as "Hopetoun"!

In the case of Kilruskin however, Isaac Jackson says that it may be from the Gaelic "riascach" meaning boggy, but is more probably from old English "riscen", meaning rushy. On that basis therefore, Kilruskin may be held to mean the "chapel of the rushes".
Certainly, Kilruskin is on the site of an old spring or well (the Dornell well), and it sits below the level of Springside which is another area well noted in local history for its boggy landscape. So the name "chapel of the rushes" would seem also to fit the topographical features of the area.

However, on the 1773 Map of Cunninhame as attached (see also the close up), the area is actually called "Kilgriskin". Old Irish "Griscin" is a reference to bones - usually a pig's spine. Was there a church of bones? It may have been an agricultural settlement based around pig famers, and the old church would be dedicated to the profession. Certainly, to drive pigs from Kilruskin into the town where the marketplace was held (the slaughterhouse was the old dairy as it is in so many towns in Scotland - now Helen Armstrong's shop) between the Barony Church and Kirktonhall.

It's one of these local mysteries we will probably never solve - but once again we should out any fanciful notion of a Saint Ruskin out of our heads.

The Reviews

Over the past few weeks, I have received many hundreds of messages and congratulations regarding the content of the "Being West Kilbride" Facebook Group. I am overwhelmed. These are just some of them:

Stephen we don't know each other but I just wanted to thank you! My mum has a terminal illness and sadly doesn't have a lot of time left. I was showing her photos from your page today and for the first time in months she had an interest in something! Seeing photos of the village and people she knew from church gave her joy! Thank you

(Private Message)

What this site has made me think is how lucky we all are to have somewhere we can all think of as home and that we will always identify with and know that that is were we are from. my mrs is from nowhere really, her family moved around when she was a child . think she is a wee bit jealous when i say "im away home for a few days". i always need to go and get my fix every now and then, wk , portencross , the glen , the beach , lawhill and all the smashing folks i meet when i go home to tattie toon.

A.M.

I'm going to make plans to come home to West Kilbride. I think in the new year some time.

D.L.

...so thank you from the tropics, Cheers!!

R.D.

I just want to say a big thank u to everyone all ur posts are amazing and reminding me of what an amazing childhood I had growing up in west Kilbride loving it don't re!member all of them but a lot of them

G.T.

Congratulations Stephen Brown on an excellent site and to everyone visiting it for their contributions, I have had a great time today looking through the photos and memories.

A.J.

Really. A great site. Rembering my childhood days

F.F.

I absolutely love this page .. wonderful photographs and stories about the village .. keep up the good work your doing

S.D.

I am sooooo loving this page. I may have been gone for over 30 years, but my heart resounds at every post. Thank you. There is just something about West Kilbride that brings us all home. My children's first steps on sand were at Seamill. Out favourite rock pools are Seamill. Now my children are grown and I'm a Gran'ma. I want my granddaughter to be on the beach with her net, catching crayfish, looking at crabs and jellyfish, the same as I did with my children. The heart never leaves the village.

S.L.

Same here! Loving the memories. Making me quite home sick!

J.M.

Touching words Stephen Brown, in particular with people from wk and outside making bridges and bringing experiences and views of our village together for all to appreciate and lessen the divide, well done Stephen .

R.B.

My husband and I moved to this "Beautiful wee village" about 14 years ago . My daughter and son both are born and bred here and in their words " I love living here " kinda says it all !! X

C.G.

Have we all overlooked something?
A certain man, whom I didn't know till recently, set up a web page
for and about West Kilbride and their knowledge. Bet we all thought
about doing it Hats off to that man. Does anybody know his name ....

J.S.

One sure thing won't be short of a friend or two !!

J.C.

A very popular man x

O.M.

Amazing job Stephen Brown, well done! Andy hates FB but your
page kept him awake into the wee small hours

C.M.

Absolutely loving all these old photos of West Kilbride and learning
a bit about our local history! Fascinating. Thank you

G.M.

Just home on leave from the Congo in Africa., and have been
enjoying looking at the old photos of wk.

K.D.

Stephen Brown, again I must thank you for this inspirational group.
It helps bridge the gap of time and miles for people like myself who
long to be there.

C.O.

About The Author

Stephen Brown, son of Albert Brown who grew up in Portencross, originally trained as an accountant but now owns and operates several diverse businesses on the west coast of Scotland.

He grew up and has lived in West Kilbride most of his life. He is passionate about his home village and its history. Over the years he has tried to play an active part in its development and regeneration.

He is a passionate collector of artefacts and documents that relate to the history of West Kilbride. He also collects specialist artistic pieces and other memorabilia, which might otherwise be lost to society. This is called the "Yerton Collection", named after the Yerton Pottery building on the main street that he once owned.

Stephen is a polymath with an interest in a large and diverse range of subjects. He is a church elder and active at the Presbytery level. A son of the desert (Laurel and Hardy fan club), Chair of Scottish Mausoleum, a member of the Friends of the Glasgow Necropolis and the Ayrshire Archaeology and Natural History Society and a Director of North Ayrshire Citizen's Advice.

Stephen has written an international bestselling book on internet gaming. He has written two books on local history and a small volume of poetry.

He is married to Catherine and together they have four children.

Other Books By Stephen Brown

All books published by The Transparent
Publishing Company

Sales@transparentpublishing.co.uk

ISBN	Title	Version
9780956208699	A History of the West Kilbride Town Crest	eBook
9781909805019	A History of the West Kilbride Town Crest	Paperback
9781909805033	A Clash of Clans Leadership Handbook	Paperback
9781909805132	A Clash of Clans Leadership Handbook	eBook
9781909805156	A Desiderata for the 21st Century	Paperback
9781909805163	A Desiderata for the 21st Century	eBook
9781909805217	Clash of Clans, Defending for Trophies	Paperback
9781909805224	Clash of Clans, Defending for Trophies	eBook
9781909805170	Being at the Top of Clash of Clans	Paperback
9781909805187	Being at the Top of Clash of Clans	eBook
9781909805323	The Portencross Armada Conspiracy	Paperback
9781909805330	The Portencross Armada Conspiracy	eBook
9781909805231	Georgian Edinburgh (Short Booklet)	Paperback
9781514722442	Georgian Edinburgh (Expected Jan 2016)	Paperback

Made in the USA
Charleston, SC
09 January 2016